Christmas Handcrafts

W9-CZT-615

Oxmoor House®

Christmas Handcrafts

©1992 by Oxmoor House, Inc.
Book Division of Southern Progress Corporation
P.O. Box 2463
Birmingham, Alabama 35201

Published by Oxmoor House, Inc., Leisure Arts, Inc., and
Symbol of Excellence Publishers, Inc.

All rights reserved. No part of this book may be reproduced in
any form or by any means without the prior written permission
of the publisher, excepting brief quotations in connection
with reviews written specifically for inclusion in a magazine or
newspaper.

All designs that appear in this book are the property of Oxmoor
House, Inc.

Library of Congress Catalog Card Number: 92-60993
Hardcover ISBN: 0-8487-1120-3
Softcover ISBN: 0-8487-1170-X
Manufactured in the United States of America
Second Printing 1993

Editor-in-Chief: Nancy J. Fitzpatrick
Director of Manufacturing: Jerry Higdon
Production Manager: Rick Litton
Associate Production Manager: Theresa L. Beste
Production Assistant: Pam Beasley Bullock
Editor: Cecilia C. Robinson

Symbol of Excellence Publishers, Inc. Staff

Editors: Barbara Cockerham, Phyllis Hoffman
Associate Editor: Diane Kennedy-Jackson
Copy Editor: Lorna Reeves
Production Manager: Wayne Hoffman
Creative Director: Mac Jamieson
Art Director: Yukie McLean
Associate Production Manager: Perry James
Editorial Assistants: Cindy Housel, Carol Odom
Staff Artists: Scott Begley, Charles Long, Michael Whisenant
Senior Photography Stylist: Tracey M. Runnion

If you believe the very best things are those which are fashioned with the hands, this collection of stitchery and craft ideas will be your inspiration for countless hours of creativity! From classic cross stitch and heirloom quilting to crafting with paper, fabric scraps, and natural materials from the woods, there's something within these pages for everyone who loves stitching, crafting, and the yuletide season!

Included in this compendium of delightful designs are projects you'll love making for family members and dear friends as well as for your own home. As you turn the pages, imagine the beautiful decorations you'll display and the wonderful gifts you'll present to each special someone on your holiday list. Then get set for many enjoyable hours of stitching and crafting pleasure and watch eyes light up with joy on Christmas morn as the lucky recipients open their treasures, handmade with love!

Contents

TRIM THE TREE

The Christmas tree, that gently scented evergreen which occupies a place of honor in most American homes throughout the holiday season, holds magical appeal for children of all ages. Perhaps no other Christmas symbol evokes as many memories and emotions as this towering giant, adorned with twinkling lights, sparkling tinsel, and a hodgepodge of colorful ornaments. And all those tiny ornaments, whether stitched, crafted, or crocheted, possess their own special charm. They even have the power to bring to mind recollections unique to each family member of special times spent together and favorite Christmases from the past.

Festive Trimmings

Ornaments are simply wonderful! From handmade to store-bought, the choices are almost endless. Whether your idea of the perfectly adorned tree is one embellished with meticulously placed trimmers, balanced to form an artistic masterpiece among the branches of a sturdy pine, or one where the entire tree is heavily laden with pieces featuring a rainbow of Christmas colors from the very tip top to the lowest bough, it is the ornaments, above all else, which make it so unique.

Some purchased pieces, acquired on family vacations, may stand as reminders of a summer getaway to the beach or perhaps of a trip to the mountains. But handmade ornaments are usually the ones which will command a second look and a favorable comment from visitors and are the ones family members hold most dear. Whether an ornament was crafted for Mom by the tiny hands of a proud and loving kindergartner or was someone's first attempt at learning to cross stitch or crochet, every ornament is special. Featured on this and the following pages in this chapter are collections of ornaments that call for a variety of handiwork skills.

Looking for something a little different for your tree? The *Christmas Bead Ornaments*, below, feature an assortment of popular holiday motifs created by adding beads with a half cross stitch. The wonder of these projects is their versatility. Use them as ornaments, refrigerator magnets, gift tags, lapel pins, and more, by simply varying the finishing techniques used!

Holiday Memories Ornaments, pictured at right, will carry the warmth of the season wherever they're placed. For those who have been collecting tree-trimming treasures for many years and who have run out of room for any more on the Christmas tree, why not cross stitch this matched dozen to display on greenery hung on a protected door? Finish as lightly stuffed "pillows" and cover the edges with cording made from matching floss.

Left—Christmas Bead Ornaments *are easily accomplished. The charts read just like those used for cross stitch—perforated paper is substituted for fabric, and the glass beads are secured with floss. Simply follow the charts and instructions, beginning on page 18, to create these holiday dazzlers.*

Opposite—Holiday Memories Ornaments *combine cross-stitch, easy finishing, and cording to create a delightful dozen for seasonal decorating. Charts begin on page 20. Instructions for making cording are on page 140.*

Simple and elegant describe the heavenly *Copper Angels And Ornaments* decorations shown on this page! The angels, cut from a flat sheet of copper foil, are formed into three-dimensional Christmas heralds by bending the skirt portion back and overlapping the ends on the back side. Shown both as a tree topper and as a mantel decoration, this easy-to-craft item features many uses—let your imagination be your guide. The small ornaments are cut from copper foil sheets and are decorated with holes punched around the perimeters. A glaze made of oil paint and paint thinner completes these coppery Christmas designs.

An all-white tree is, in a word, spectacular. Shown on the evergreen at right is a truly exquisite collection of ornaments, cross stitched in white with silver and gold accents. Accompanying them are delicate crocheted snowflakes that, in addition to lending the perfect finishing touch to this all-white evergreen, will add charm to a tree decorated in the more traditional red and green. Add several strings of tiny white lights to enhance your needlework and let the Christmas tree signal the beginning of a festive season!

Left top and bottom—Copper Angels And Ornaments *can be crafted with ease from copper foil sheets, available at craft stores. Instructions begin on page 16.*

Opposite—The White Christmas Ornaments *are wonderful for making a formal statement. The cross-stitch pieces feature a flat-finishing technique; and the crocheted snowflakes, created with a ball of thread and a small crochet hook, make great remembrances to tuck into Christmas cards! Charts begin on page 26. Crochet instructions are on page 15.*

TRIM THE TREE
Festive Trimmings

Trimming the tree with prized decorations is one of the most exciting annual events in many homes during the yuletide season. Another holiday practice, that of sending and receiving Christmas cards and letters, ranks high on the list of seasonal delights. When the card includes an ornament tucked carefully inside, these two traditions come together

beautifully! Begin a yearly custom with friends and relatives by including small, flat keepsakes, such as these *"Quilted" Remembrances Paper Ornaments*, inside your greetings to them.

Searching for a creative use for those scraps of ribbon that are just a little bit too long to throw away? Re-create ribbon candy, a favorite sweet treat at Christmas, by using fancy ribbon and fabric stiffener. Unlike the real thing, these *Ribbon Candy Ornaments* are for decorating the tree, so they add no calories!

On this page—For mailbox greetings that are certain to be remembered, include these "Quilted" Remembrances Paper Ornaments with the Christmas cards you send to relatives and good friends. Craft popular holiday "sweets" from assorted ribbon scraps to make delightful Ribbon Candy Ornaments. Instructions are on page 14.

Who would have guessed that eggs could be so adorable? Of course these aren't the real thing—they're actually plastic craft ovals combined with paints to make *Egg Santa Ornaments*. Whether crafting these adorable Saint Nicks with plastic eggs or with the more expensive wooden kind, get set for plenty of free-time fun while painting these jolly, lovable characters, which are simply precious for adorning the holiday tree!

Egg Santa Ornaments

Materials:

Plastic or wooden craft eggs (one for **each** ornament you wish to make)
White chenille balls (one for **each** ornament you wish to make)
Gesso acrylic undercoating
Acrylic paints: red, green, white, black, gold, fleshtone
Assorted paintbrushes
Graphite paper
Craft glue
Pencil
Metallic gold thread, cut into 5" lengths (for hangers)
Needle   Scissors

1. Paint craft eggs with two coats gesso, allowing to dry between coats.
2. Use pattern, graphite paper, and pencil to trace outline of head, beard, moustache, and mittens onto each egg.
Note: It is easier to freehand nose, eyes, cheeks, etc.
3. Paint all areas red except beard, moustache, face, mittens, and edge of cap. It will take two coats to cover completely.
4. Mix black and white paints to make gray. Paint beard gray. Let dry and paint beard white, using small, comma-like strokes. Paint cuffs and edge of cap white.
5. Paint face area fleshtone. Paint eyes black. Mix red and white to make pink. Paint nose, cheeks, and mouth pink. Paint eyebrows white.
6. Paint mittens green.
7. Outline arms using black. Paint belt front and back black. Paint buckle gold.
8. Outline mustache, beard, cap, and mittens using black.
9. Glue white chenille ball to top of cap. Let dry. Thread needle with a 5" length of gold metallic thread, sew through chenille ball, and tie a loop in thread ends to form hanger.

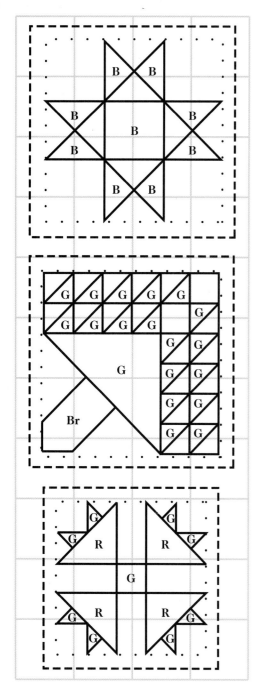

1 square = 1"

"Quilted" Remembrances Paper Ornaments

Materials:
4" square of 140 lb. watercolor paper (for **each** ornament)
Americana™ acrylic paints: True Blue, Dark Pine Green, Dark Chocolate, Calico Red
12"-length metallic gold thread (for **each** hanger)
Graphite paper **or** #2 pencil and typing paper
Sewing machine **or** tracing wheel **or** sharp needle
Artist's paintbrush with a sharp edge (designer used a ⅛" "Rose Petal" brush by Loew-Cornell)
Ruler
Hand-sewing needle
Scissors

1. Enlarge patterns as indicated. Place graphite paper colored-side down on watercolor paper and, using a ruler, trace quilt patterns onto watercolor paper. (Graphite paper is generally available at art supply stores. If unavailable in your area, you can make your own by rubbing the lead of a #2 pencil over one side of a piece of typing paper.)
2. Fill in shapes as indicated on patterns, using acrylic paint. Let dry.
3. With sewing machine **UNTHREADED**, sew along dotted lines to suggest quilting. If a sewing machine is unavailable, roll a tracing wheel along dotted lines or use a sharp needle to make holes.
4. Thread needle with gold thread, pierce one corner of ornament with needle, and pull thread through hole. Tie a knot in thread ends to form hanger.

```
– – – = Cutting Lines
. . . . = "Quilting" Lines
    R = Calico Red
    G = Dark Pine Green
   Br = Dark Chocolate
    B = True Blue
```

Ribbon Candy Ornaments

Materials:
⅝"- to ¾"-wide assorted striped craft ribbons in Christmas colors, cut into 12" strips
1½"-wide assorted striped craft ribbons in Christmas colors, cut into 24" strips
Silver thread, cut into 7" lengths (for hangers)
Liquid fabric stiffener
Flat plastic foam (to pin ribbons on while they dry)
Waxed paper
Paintbrush
Rustproof, fine straight pins
Measuring tape
Sharp hand-sewing needle
Scissors
Pliers (optional)

Note: Cover work surface with waxed paper before beginning—this is messy!

1. Following directions on fabric stiffener bottle, paint stiffener on both sides of one piece of ribbon, smoothing with paintbrush for an even coat. Pin through center of ribbon into plastic foam, forming curls as shown in illustration. Keep all curls tight together and the same height, approximately ¾" high for narrow ribbons and 1" high for wide ribbons. Ease pinned ribbon slightly away from plastic foam so stiffener won't adhere ribbon to plastic foam. Repeat for **each** ornament you wish to make.
2. Let ornaments dry overnight or until thoroughly dry. Remove pins from ribbon. (You may wish to use pliers to save your fingers!)
3. Trim one end of ribbon curl into a point. Thread needle with 7" length silver thread, stitch through ribbon near tip of point, and tie a knot in thread ends to form hanger. Repeat for remaining ornaments.

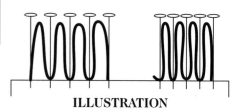

ILLUSTRATION

White Christmas—Crochet

```
CROCHET ABBREVIATIONS
ch—chain
dc—double crochet
sc—single crochet
sl st—slip stitch
sp—space
tr—treble crochet
(*)—repeat from * to *
```

Materials:
225 yd. ball white bedspread weight crochet cotton, size 10
Size 8 steel crochet hook
Clear nylon monofilament, cut into 8" lengths (for hangers)
Plastic foam board
Rustproof pins
Fabric stiffener **or** white glue and water

Helpful Information: Each snowflake measures 5" to 6". For better tension control, wind the thread an extra time around your little or ring finger. At the beginning of the row, ch 3 counts as a dc; ch 4 counts as a tr. To finish, cut end threads 2" long and weave through back of stitches. Trim ends. To stiffen snowflakes after finishing crochet, saturate them in fabric stiffener or in a 2 to 1 solution of fresh white glue and water. Gently squeeze out excess. For drying, lay waxed paper over a plastic foam board, and use **rustproof** pins to attach snowflakes to board. Make sure the arms of each snowflake form straight lines. Dry thoroughly. Use a fan or hair dryer to speed drying, if desired. Weave an 8"-length of monofilament through one arm of each flake and tie monofilament ends together to form hangers.

Uses: Decorate holiday trees, packages, greeting cards, windowpanes, and wreaths. Suspend from a chandelier or make a mobile.

Snowflake A: Ch 6, sl st in 1st ch to form ring. Row 1: In ring make sc, (ch 8, sc, ch 6, sc) 6 times, except instead of final ch 6, sc, make ch 3, dc in 1st sc [counts as ch 6 sp]. Row 2: Sc in sp just made, (ch 8, sc in next ch 6 sp) 6 times except instead of final sc make sl st in 1st sc and ch. Row 3: Ch 3, (in same sp make 2 dc, ch 3, 3 dc, ch 3; dc in next sp) 6 times, except instead of final dc, make sl st in 3rd ch and 2 dc. Row 4: (In next sp make sc, ch 3, sc; in next sp make 3 dc, ch 10, 3 dc) 6 times, sl st in 1st sc and ch. Row 5: Sc in sp, (ch 9, 2 tr in 4th ch from hook, ch 6, sl st in last tr [= tip], ch 4, 2 tr in same tr as tip, ch 5, sc in same ch 3 sp on row 4, ch 1; in ch 10 sp make 9 dc, ch 5, 9 dc, ch 1; sc in next ch 3 sp) 6 times, except instead of final sc, make sl st in 1st sc. Finish.

Snowflake B: Ch 5, sl st in 1st ch to form ring. Row 1: (Sc in ring, ch 6) 6 times, sl st in 1st sc and sp. Row 2: Ch 3, dc in sp, (ch 5, 2 dc in same sp, 2 dc in next sp) 6 times, except instead of final 2 dc, make sl st in 3rd ch, dc and sp. Row 3: Ch 4, tr, ch 10, 2 tr in same sp, ch 7; (in next sp make 2 tr, ch 10, 2 tr, ch 7) 5 times, sl st in 4th ch, tr and sp. Row 4: Ch 4, (in same ch 10 sp make 7 tr, ch 9, tr in 4th ch from hook, ch 6, sl st in last tr [= tip], ch 4, tr in same tr as tip, ch 5, sl st in last tr in ch 10 sp below, 8 tr in same sp; in ch 7 sp make sc, ch 4, tr in last sc, ch 6, sl st in last tr, ch 4, tr in same tr, sc in same ch 7 sp; tr in next sp) 6 times, except instead of final tr make sl st in 4th ch. Finish.

Snowflake C: Ch 6, sl st in 1st ch to form ring. Row 1: In ring make sc, (ch 10, sc, ch 5, sc) 6 times, except instead of final ch 5, sc, make ch 2, dc in 1st sc [counts as ch 5 sp]. Row 2: Ch 3, dc in sp just made, (ch 10, in next ch 5 sp make 2 dc) 5 times; ch 10, sl st in 3rd ch at beginning of row. Row 3: Ch 5, (in next sp make 5 dc, ch 10, 5 dc, ch 1) 6 times, except instead of final dc, ch 1, make sl st in 3rd ch and sp. Row 4: Ch 3, dc in same sp, (ch 4, in next sp make 7 dc, ch 8, 7 dc; ch 4, in ch 1 sp make 2 dc) 6 times, except instead of final 2 dc, make sl st in 3rd ch and dc. Row 5: (4 sc in next sp, ch 5; in next sp make 3 dc, ch 4, sl st in last dc, 3 dc, ch 15, sl st in last dc [= tip], 3 dc, ch 4, sl st in last dc, 3 dc; ch 5, in next sp make 4 sc, ch 4, sl st in last sc) 6 times, sl st in 1st sc. Finish.

Snowflake D: Ch 5, sl st in 1st ch to form ring. Row 1: (Sc in ring, ch 6) 5 times, sc in ring, ch 2, tr in 1st sc [counts as ch 6 sp]. Row 2: Ch 3, dc in sp just made, (2 dc in next sp, ch 8, 2 dc in same sp) 5 times; in next sp make 2 dc, ch 4, tr in 3rd ch at beginning of row. Row 3: Sc in sp just made, (ch 4, 2 tr in last sc, ch 4, 2 tr in last tr, ch 10, sl st in last tr, ch 4, 2 tr in same tr, ch 4, 2 tr in last tr, sc in next ch 8 sp; ch 4, tr in last sc, ch 4, tr in last tr, ch 12, sl st in last tr [= tip], ch 4, tr in same tr, ch 4, tr in last tr, sc in same ch 8 sp) 6 times, sl st in 1st sc. Finish.

Snowflake E: Ch 6, sl st in 1st ch to form ring. Row 1: In ring make sc, (ch 10, sc, ch 5, sc) 6 times, except instead of final ch 5, sc, make ch 2, dc in 1st sc [counts as ch 5 sp]. Row 2: Ch 3, dc in sp just made, (ch 10, in next ch 5 sp make 2 dc) 5 times; ch 10, sl st in 3rd ch at beginning of row. Row 3: Ch 5, (in next sp make 5 dc, ch 10, 5 dc, ch 2) 6 times, except instead of final dc, ch 2, make sl st in 3rd ch. Row 4: (In next sp make sc, ch 3, sc, ch 5; in next sp make sc, ch 10, sc, ch 5) 6 times, sl st in 1st sc and sp. Row 5: *Ch 2, 2 dc in same ch 3 sp, (ch 3, 2 dc in last dc) 3 times; in next ch 10 sp make 2 dc, (ch 3, 2 dc in last dc) 3 times, 2 dc in same ch 10 sp; (ch 3, 2 dc in last dc) 4 times, sc in next ch 3 sp.* Repeat * 5 times, except instead of final sc, make sl st in 1st ch. Finish.

Snowflake F: Ch 6, sl st in 1st ch to form ring. Row 1: Ch 3, 17 dc in ring, sl st to 3rd ch at beginning of row. Row 2: Ch 4, tr in next dc, (ch 10, skip 1 dc, tr in next 2 dc) 5 times, ch 6, tr in 4th ch [counts as ch 10 sp]. Row 3: Ch 4, 2 tr in sp just made, (in next sp make ch 1, 3 tr, ch 12, 3 tr) 5 times, in next sp make 3 tr, ch 8, tr in 4th ch. Row 4: Ch 4, 2 tr in sp just made, *in ch 1 sp, make 2 tr; in next ch 12 sp make (3 tr, ch 3) 3 times, 3 tr.* Repeat * 5 times, except instead of final 3 tr, make sl st in 4th ch. Row 5: *Sc in next 6 tr, in next sp make (3 tr, ch 6, sl st in last tr) 2 times; in center sp make 3 tr, ch 3, tr in last tr, ch 6, sl st in last tr [= tip], tr in last tr below, ch 3, sl st in same tr below, 3 tr in same center sp; ch 6, sl st in last tr, in next sp make 3 tr, ch 6, sl st in last tr, 3 tr; skip tr.* Repeat * 5 times, sl st in 1st sc. Finish.

Snowflake G: Ch 6, sl st in 1st ch to form ring. Row 1: Ch 3, 17 dc in ring, sl st in 3rd ch. Row 2: (Sc in next 3 dc, ch 8) 6 times, except instead of final ch 8 make ch 4, tr in 1st sc. Row 3: Sc in sp just made, *ch 3, dc in last sc, (ch 3, dc in last dc) 2 times, in next sp make sc, ch 2, sc.* Repeat * 5 times, except instead of final sc make sl st in 1st sc and ch. Row 4: Sc in same sp, *ch 3, dc in last sc, (ch 3, dc in last dc) 3 times; ch 5, sl st in last dc, ch 8, sl st in same dc, ch 5, sl st in same dc; (ch 3, dc in last dc) 4 times; skip 1 ch 3 sp on row 3, sc in next sp, sc in ch 2 sp, ch 10, sl st in 4th ch from hook, ch 6, sc in same ch 2 sp, sc in next ch 3 sp.* Repeat * 5 times, except instead of final sc, make sl st in 1st sc. Finish.

Snowflake H: Ch 5, sl st in 1st ch to form ring. Row 1: Ch 4, tr in ring, *(ch 4, tr in last tr) 3 times, 2 tr in ring.* Repeat * 5 times, except instead of final 2 tr, make sl st in 4th ch, tr and ch. Row 2: Sc in sp, (ch 4, tr in next sp, ch 8, tr in same sp, ch 4, sc in next sp, sc in next ch 4 sp) 6 times, except instead of final sc, make sl st in 1st sc. Row 3: (4 sc in next sp; in next sp make 5 sc, ch 3, dc in last sc, ch 11, sl st in 10th ch from hook, ch 9, sl st in 8th ch, ch 7, sl st in 6th ch, ch 6, sl st in 5th ch, ch 6, sl st in same ch [= tip], ch 5, sl st in same ch, ch 7, sl st in 6th ch, ch 9, sl st in 8th ch, ch 11, sl st in 10th ch, sl st in same ch as 1st ch 11 sl st, ch 1, sl st in dc below, ch 3, sl st in last sc, 5 sc in same sp; 4 sc in next sp, ch 10, sl st in 4th ch from hook, ch 6, sl st in last sc) 6 times, sl st in 1st sc. Finish.

Copper Ornaments

Materials:

Two 9" x 12" sheets copper foil (available at craft stores)
5" x 5" square of soft wood
Ceramcoat® Water Base Varnish
Burnt umber oil paint
Odorless oil paint thinner
½"-wide paintbrush
3½ yds. gold metallic thread, cut into 7" lengths (for hangers)
Extra fine sandpaper
Measuring tape
Small nail
Hammer
Soft rags
Pencil **or** stylus
Old scissors

Note: Materials listed will make eighteen ornaments (five birds, six stars, three houses, and four angels).

1. Sand flat surface of copper foil sheets. Cut out patterns and trace onto sheets, using pencil **or** stylus. (Since foil is soft, an indentation can be made easily with either one.) Cut out designs and mark dots.

2. Place each ornament on wood and use hammer and nail to make small holes in ornament, following marked dots.

3. Dip rag into thinner and then into oil paint and cover each ornament with mixture. Let dry until dull. Beginning at center, wipe off glaze, leaving dark around edges. Let dry overnight.

4. Apply a coat of Ceramcoat® Water Base Varnish. Let dry.

5. Run a 7"-piece metallic gold thread through hole at top of **each** ornament and tie a knot in thread ends to form hanger.

16

Copper Angel

Materials:

8½" x 11" piece 40-gauge copper tooling foil (for **each** angel)
8½" x 11" piece red felt (for **each** angel)
9" x 12" piece soft wood

Ceramcoat® Water Base Varnish
Burnt umber oil paint
Odorless oil paint thinner
½"-wide paintbrush
Extra fine sandpaper
Small nail
Hammer

Soft rags
Pencil **or** stylus
Old scissors
Craft glue

1. Sand flat surface of copper tooling foil. Cut out pattern and trace onto foil using pencil **or** stylus. (Since foil is soft, an indentation can be made easily with either one.) Cut out angel and mark dots.

2. Place angel on wood and use hammer and nail to make small holes in angel, following marked dots.

3. Dip rag into thinner and then into oil paint and apply a light coat of mixture over angel. Let dry until dull. Beginning at center, wipe off glaze, leaving dark around edges. Let dry overnight.

4. Glue felt to back of angel. Trim felt.

5. Brush a coat of varnish on angel front. Let dry.

6. Fold skirt back below wings, overlapping as indicated on pattern. Glue at overlap.

7. Repeat for **each** angel.

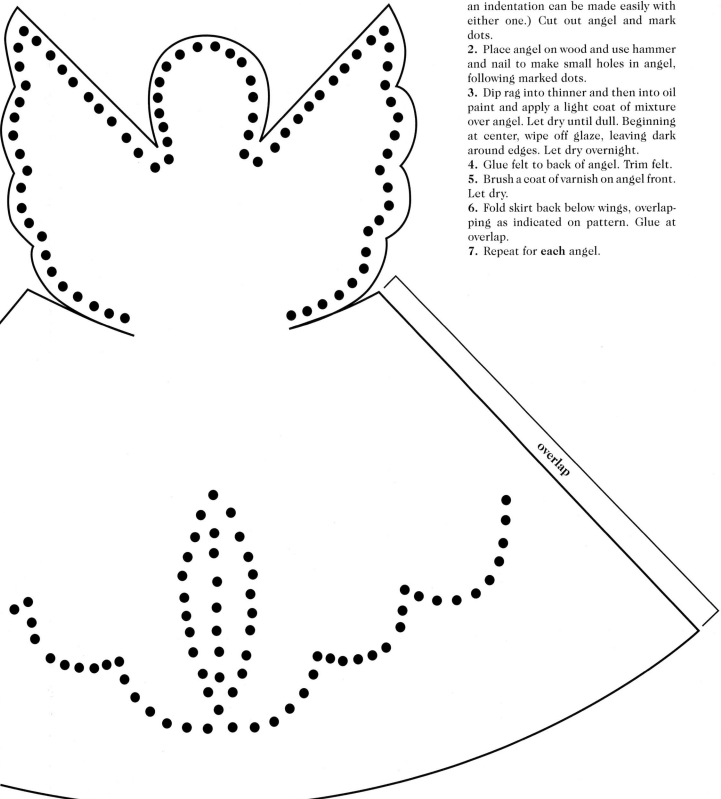

overlap

Christmas Bead Ornaments

Mill Hill Glass Seed Beads

•	00479	white
■	00081	jet
∕	00150	gray
×	00221	bronze
−	00128	yellow
▲	00332	emerald
6	00167	Christmas green
o	00165	Christmas red
3	00367	garnet
⊙	00145	pink
+	00143	robin egg blue
\	00148	pale peach
❘	00123	cream
v	00557	gold
✳	02011	Victorian gold
c	00358	cobalt blue
=	00275	coral
α	00283	mercury
z	02006	ice blue
∟	00968	red

Gingerbread House
Material: 14-count white perforated paper from Craft World International®, Inc.
Stitch count: 40H x 24W
Design size:
14-count   2⅞" x 1¾"
Floss: DMC white

Santa's Elf
Material: 14-count buff perforated paper from Craft World International®, Inc.
Stitch count: 38H x 25W

Design size:
14-count   2¾" x 1¾"
Floss: DMC 738 tan, vy. lt.

Christmas Tree
Material: 14-count green perforated paper from Craft World International®, Inc.
Stitch count: 36H x 23W
Design size:
14-count   2⅝" x 1⅝"
Floss: DMC 911 emerald, med.

Angel and Horn
Material: 14-count buff perforated paper from Craft World International®, Inc.
Stitch count: 26H x 49W
Design size:
14-count   1⅞" x 3½"
Floss: DMC 738 tan, vy. lt.

Bell and Bow
Material: 14-count silver perforated paper from Craft World International®, Inc.
Stitch count: 30H x 30W
Design size:
14-count   2⅛" x 2⅛"
Floss: DMC 762 pearl gray, vy. lt.

Noel and Hearts
Material: 14-count red perforated paper from Craft World International®, Inc.
Stitch count: 30H x 30W
Design size:
14-count   2⅛" x 2⅛"
Floss: DMC 304 red, med.

Snowman
Material: 14-count white perforated paper from Craft World International®, Inc.
Stitch count: 34H x 22W
Design size:
14-count   2⅜" x 1⅝"
Floss: DMC white

Angel and Candle
Material: 14-count gold perforated paper from Craft World International®, Inc.
Stitch count: 30H x 30W
Design size:
14-count   2⅛" x 2⅛"
Floss: DMC 676 old gold, lt.

Instructions: Separate floss into single strands. Begin work at upper left or right corner of design. Work counted-bead embroidery with a half cross stitch, securing thread on back as for regular cross stitch. Begin each half cross in lower-left hole, attach a bead, and finish half cross diagonally in upper-right hole, referring to illustration on page 19.
Note: The size of each bead may vary. Bead will slant in opposite direction from half cross. The designs may be worked from left to right or from right to left. In order for the beads to lay properly, the entire design must be worked in one direction; and each row must be completed before beginning the next. As you stitch, the last bead added may seem loose. Beginning the next stitch will tighten it. Maintain an even tension and rhythm as you work the design, as these

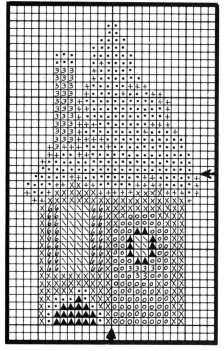

GINGERBREAD HOUSE

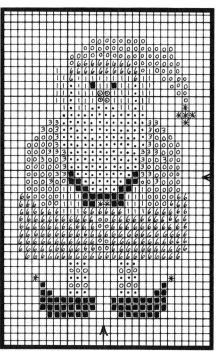

SANTA'S ELF

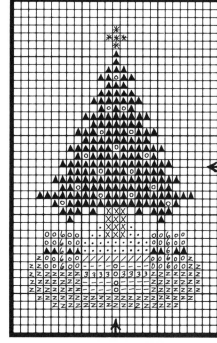

CHRISTMAS TREE

are important to the appearance of the finished product. If three or more stitches must be skipped, secure thread first on the back side. If a row of beads looks crooked when it is completed, run the thread through the line of beads to straighten it. To finish as an ornament, cut out shape one hole outside stitched area, being careful not to clip working threads. Attach decorative loop on back of ornament for hanging.

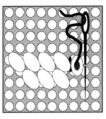

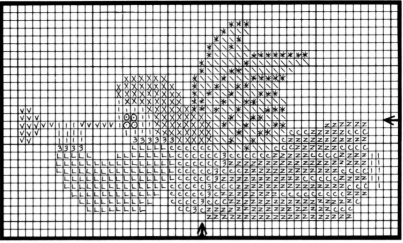

ANGEL AND HORN

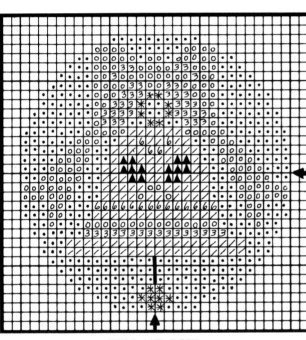

BELL AND BOW

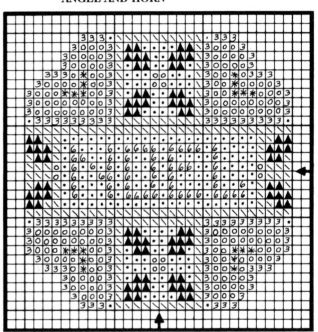

NOEL AND HEARTS

SNOWMAN

ANGEL AND CANDLE

19

Holiday Memories Ornaments—
Under The Tree (Girls)

	DMC	Color
●	3371	black-brown
=	948	peach flesh, vy. lt.
S	761	salmon, lt. (half cross)
·	white	white
V	415	pearl gray
X	826	blue, med.
Z	825	blue, dk.
╱	ecru	ecru
L	822	beige-gray, lt.
T	677	old gold, vy. lt.
C	676	old gold, lt.
H	729	old gold, med.
e	321	red
J	498	red, med.
7	604	cranberry, lt.
E	603	cranberry
‖	704	chartreuse, bt.
3	701	green, lt.
o	700	green, bt.
M	3328	salmon, dk.
◢	801	coffee brown, dk.
⌒	3024	brown-gray, vy. lt.

Fabric: 18-count ivory Aida from Zweigart®
Stitch count: 46H x 46W
Design size:

11-count	4¼" x 4¼"	14-count	3¼" x 3¼"
18-count	2½" x 2½"	22-count	2⅛" x 2⅛"

Instructions: Cross stitch using two strands of floss. Backstitch using one strand 3371.

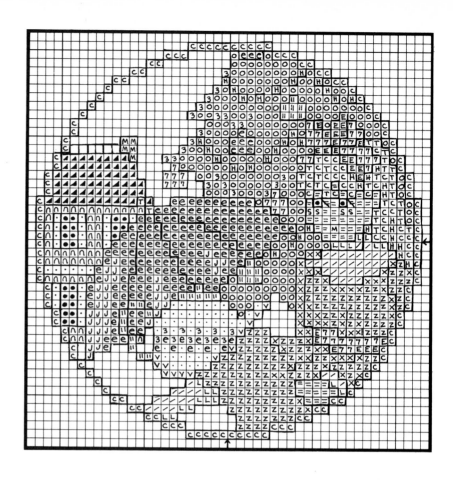

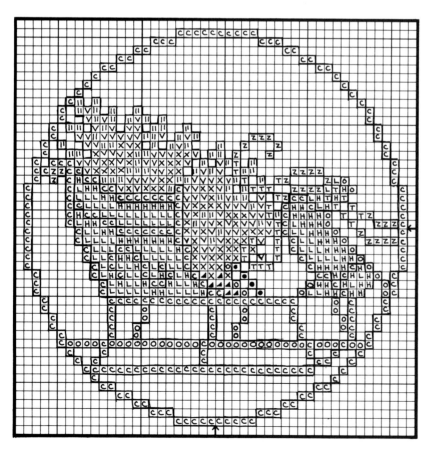

Holiday Sleigh

	DMC	Color
C	676	old gold, lt.
o	729	old gold, med.
L	321	red
H	498	red, dk.
‖	702	kelly green
V	701	green, lt.
X	699	green
●	801	coffee brown, dk.
T	434	brown, lt.
Z	435	brown, vy. lt.
◢	815	garnet, med.
bs	3371	black-brown

Fabric: 18-count ivory Aida from Zweigart®
Stitch count: 46H x 46W
Design size:

11-count	4¼" x 4¼"
14-count	3¼" x 3¼"
18-count	2½" x 2½"
22-count	2⅛" x 2⅛"

Instructions: Cross stitch using two strands of floss. Backstitch (bs) using one strand 3371.

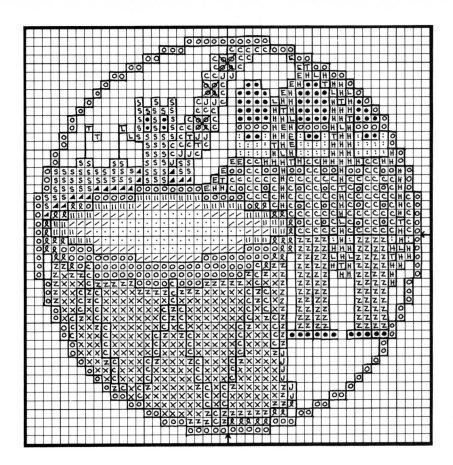

Under The Tree (Boys)

	DMC	Color
●	3371	black-brown
C	321	red
J	498	red, dk.
L	604	cranberry, lt.
o	676	old gold, lt.
ℓ	729	old gold, med.
X	826	blue, med.
Z	825	blue, dk.
:	951	flesh, vy. lt.
T	704	chartreuse, bt.
E	701	green, lt.
H	700	green, bt.
‖	822	beige-gray, lt.
∕	822	beige-gray, lt. (half cross)
•	white	white
S	648	beaver gray, lt.
▲	646	beaver gray, dk.

Fabric: 18-count ivory Aida from Zweigart®
Stitch count: 46H x 46W
Design size:

11-count	4¼" x 4¼"
14-count	3¼" x 3¼"
18-count	2½" x 2½"
22-count	2⅛" x 2⅛"

Instructions: Cross stitch using two strands of floss. Backstitch using one strand 3371.

Rocking Horse

	DMC	Color
C	321	red
L	604	cranberry, lt.
Z	676	old gold, lt.
•	437	tan, lt.
=	436	tan
7	435	brown, vy. lt.
X	433	brown, med.
V	801	coffee brown, dk.
T	704	chartreuse, bt.
●	3371	black-brown
H	700	green, bt.
E	701	green, lt.
J	498	red, dk.
S	815	garnet, med.

Fabric: 18-count ivory Aida from Zweigart®
Stitch count: 46H x 46W
Design size:

11-count	4¼" x 4¼"
14-count	3¼" x 3¼"
18-count	2½" x 2½"
22-count	2⅛" x 2⅛"

Instructions: Cross stitch using two strands of floss. Backstitch using one strand 3371.

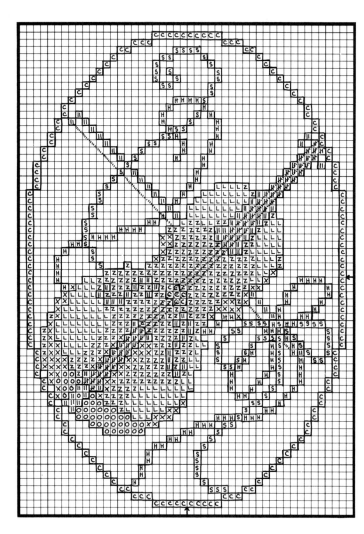

Violin

	DMC	Color
II	3371	black-brown
C	676	old gold, lt.
O	801	coffee brown, dk.
X	434	brown, lt.
Z	435	brown, vy. lt.
L	436	tan
S	321	red
H	701	green, lt.
bs	762	pearl gray, vy. lt.

Fabric: 18-count ivory Aida from Zweigart®
Stitch count: 66H x 46W
Design size:
11-count   6" x 4¼"
14-count   4¾" x 3¼"
18-count   3⅝" x 2½"
22-count   3" x 2⅛"
Instructions: Cross stitch using two stands of floss. Backstitch using one strand of floss.
Backstitch (bs) instructions:
— 3371
IIIII 762

Hurricane Lamp

	DMC	Color
C	676	old gold, lt.
H	729	old gold, med.
O	321	red
Z	498	red, med.
X	815	garnet, med.
•	703	chartreuse
L	702	kelly green
=	701	green, lt.
3	700	green, bt.
/	762	pearl gray, vy. lt.
J	726	topaz, lt. (half cross)
Fk	603	cranberry
bs	3371	black-brown
bs	318	steel gray, lt.
bs	725	topaz

Fabric: 18-count ivory Aida from Zweigart®
Stitch count: 66H x 46W
Design size:
11-count   6" x 4¼"   14-count   4¾" x 3¼"
18-count   3⅝" x 2½"   22-count   3" x 2⅛"
Instructions: Cross stitch using two strands of floss. Backstitch using one strand. Make French knots (Fk) where ✳ appears using one strand 603, wrapping floss around needle twice.
Note: Backstitch globe on lamp before backstitching holly.
Backstitch (bs) instructions:
— 3371   ᴧᴧᴧ 725   •••• 318 (globe)

Pineapple

	DMC	Color
=	832	olive
L	702	kelly green
X	700	green, bt.
Z	699	green
o	321	red
7	498	red, med.
H	815	garnet, med.
C	676	old gold, lt.
V	729	old gold, med.
3	680	old gold, dk.
bs	3371	black-brown

Fabric: 18-count ivory Aida from Zweigart®
Stitch count: 66H x 46W
Design size:

11-count	6" x 4¼"
14-count	4¾" x 3¼"
18-count	3⅝" x 2½"
22-count	3" x 2⅛"

Instructions: Cross stitch using two strands of floss. Backstitch (bs) using one strand 3371.

Weather Vane

	DMC	Color
•	677	old gold, vy. lt.
C	676	old gold, lt.
X	729	old gold, med.
Z	680	old gold, dk.
L	321	red
T	498	red, dk.
3	702	kelly green
H	700	green, bt.
bs	3371	black-brown

Fabric: 18-count ivory Aida from Zweigart®
Stitch count: 66H x 46W
Design size:

11-count	6" x 4¼"
14-count	4¾" x 3¼"
18-count	3⅝" x 2½"
22-count	3" x 2⅛"

Instructions: Cross stitch using two stands of floss. Backstitch using one strand of floss.
Backstitch (bs) instructions:

—	3371
∧∧	680

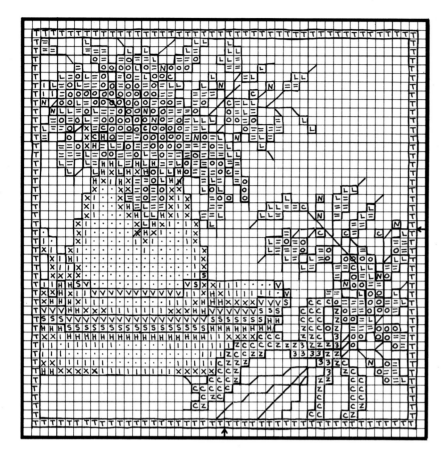

A Pot of Holly

	DMC	Color
C	321	red
Z	498	red, dk.
3	815	garnet, med.
O	701	green, lt.
=	702	kelly green
L	703	chartreuse
N	604	cranberry, lt.
V	726	topaz, lt.
S	725	topaz
•	white	white
I	762	pearl gray, vy. lt.
X	415	pearl gray (half cross)
H	415	pearl gray
T	676	old gold, lt.
bs	3371	black-brown

Fabric: 18-count ivory Aida from Zweigart®
Stitch count: 46H x 46W
Design size:

11-count	4¼" x 4¼"
14-count	3¼" x 3¼"
18-count	2½" x 2½"
22-count	2⅛" x 2⅛"

Instructions: Cross stitch using two strands of floss. Backstitch (bs) using one strand 3371.

Horn With Holly

	DMC	Color
C	321	red
T	498	red, dk.
3	815	garnet, med.
H	603	cranberry
S	435	brown, vy. lt.
•	433	brown, med.
=	703	chartreuse
O	702	kelly green
Z	700	green, bt.
·	677	old gold, vy. lt.
L	676	old gold, lt.
X	729	old gold, med.
◢	680	old gold, dk.
bs	3371	black-brown
bs	937	green, med.

Fabric: 18-count ivory Aida from Zweigart®
Stitch count: 46H x 46W
Design size:

11-count	4¼" x 4¼"	14-count	3¼" x 3¼"
18-count	2½" x 2½"	22-count	2⅛" x 2⅛"

Instructions: Cross stitch using two strands of floss. Backstitch using one strand of floss.
Backstitch (bs) instructions:
— 3371   •••• 937 (pine needles)

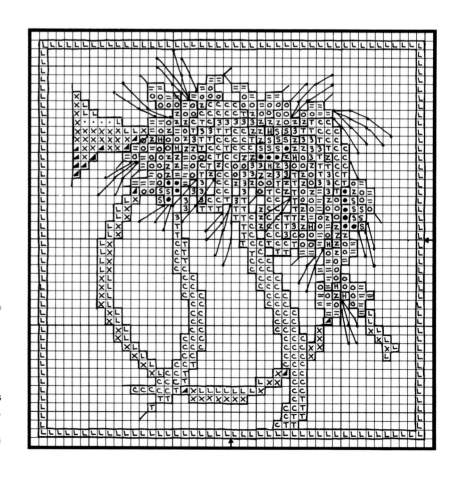

Spinning Wheel

	DMC	Color
C	676	old gold, lt.
X	729	old gold, med.
=	321	red
•	437	tan, lt.
7	436	tan
Z	435	brown, vy. lt.
S	433	brown, med.
●	3371	black-brown
e	801	coffee brown, dk.
3	498	red, dk.
L	604	cranberry, lt.
O	704	chartreuse, bt.
V	700	green, bt.
H	745	yellow, lt. pl.
◢	815	garnet, med.
╱	702	kelly green

Fabric: 18-count ivory Aida from Zweigart®
Stitch count: 46H x 46W
Design size:

11-count	4¼" x 4¼"
14-count	3¼" x 3¼"
18-count	2½" x 2½"
22-count	2⅛" x 2⅛"

Instructions: Cross stitch using two strands of floss. Backstitch using one strand of floss.
Backstitch instructions:
— 3371   •••• 704 (thread)

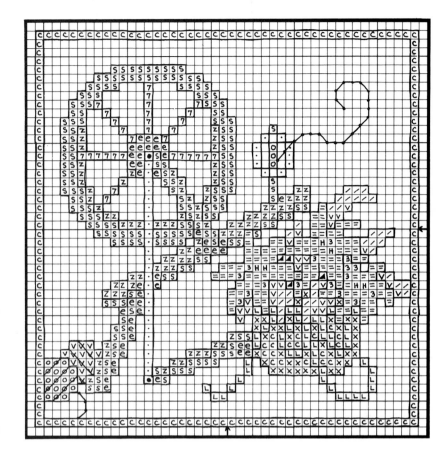

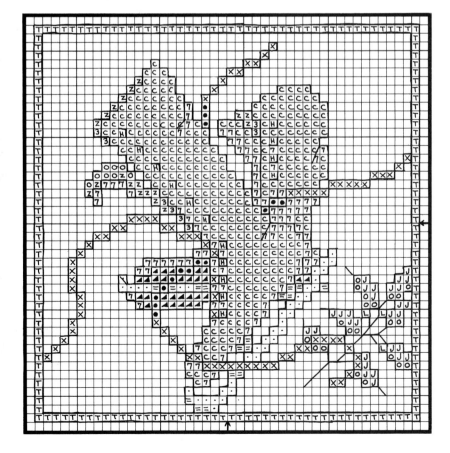

Ice Skates

	DMC	Color
X	321	red
●	498	red, dk.
L	604	cranberry, lt.
=	415	pearl gray
C	437	tan, lt.
7	436	tan
◢	801	coffee brown, dk.
•	762	pearl gray, vy. lt.
J	703	chartreuse
O	702	kelly green
Z	701	green, lt.
3	700	green, bt.
T	676	old gold, lt.
H	729	old gold, med.
bs	3371	black-brown

Fabric: 18-count ivory Aida from Zweigart®
Stitch count: 46H x 46W
Design size:

11-count	4¼" x 4¼"
14-count	3¼" x 3¼"
18-count	2½" x 2½"
22-count	2⅛" x 2⅛"

Instructions: Cross stitch using two strands of floss. Backstitch (bs) using one strand 3371.

White Christmas—Cross Stitch

	DMC	Kreinik Metallics	Color
Z	3347		yellow-green, med.
L	676		old gold, lt.
J	729		old gold, med.
X	347		salmon, dk.
●	413		pewter gray, dk.
∕	415		pearl gray
		001-BF	silver
○	676		old gold, lt.
		002-BF	gold

Fabric: 14-count white Aida from Zweigart®

Stitch count:

Silver Bells	86H x 79W
Bowing Reindeer	65H x 85W
Standing Lamb	66H x 56W
Holiday Bell	88H x 70W
Leaping Reindeer	97H x 85W
Resting Lamb	47H x 72W
Prancing Reindeer	90H x 93W
Christmas Dove-Right	77H x 55W
Poinsettia	84H x 81W
Poinsettia Duet	83H x 69W
Christmas Dove-Left	74H x 81W
Christmas Dove	55H x 96W

Design size:

Silver Bells	
14-count	6⅛" x 5⅝"
Bowing Reindeer	
14-count	4⅝" x 6⅛"
Standing Lamb	
14-count	4¾" x 4"
Holiday Bell	
14-count	6¼" x 5"
Leaping Reindeer	
14-count	6⅞" x 6⅛"
Resting Lamb	
14-count	3⅜" x 5⅛"
Prancing Reindeer	
14-count	6⅜" x 6⅝"
Christmas Dove-Right	
14-count	5½" x 3⅞"
Poinsettia	
14-count	6" x 5⅞"
Poinsettia Duet	
14-count	6" x 5"
Christmas Dove-Left	
14-count	5¼" x 5¾"
Christmas Dove	
14-count	3⅞" x 6⅞"

Instructions: Cross stitch using two strands of floss. Backstitch using three strands of floss. When blending DMC and Kreinik Metallics, use one strand of DMC and two strands of Kreinik Blending Filament.

Backstitch instructions:

···· ⌐ 676
     L 002

— ⌐ 415
    L 001

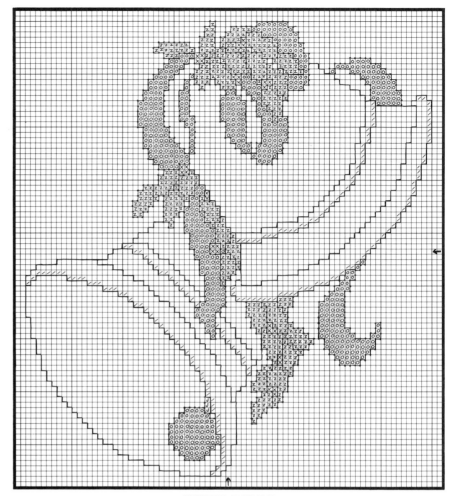

SILVER BELLS

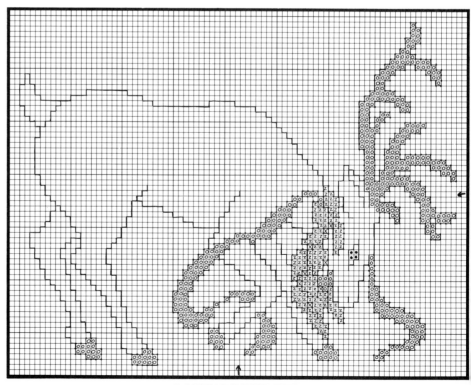

BOWING REINDEER

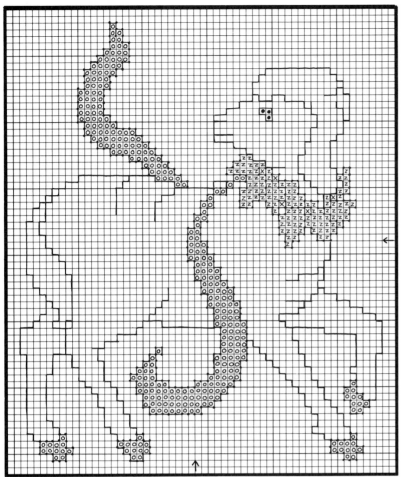

STANDING LAMB

Materials:

6 squares white felt
½ yd. 44/45"-wide Pellon® Wonder-Under™ fusible web
Dritz® Fray-Check™
Balger® gold blending filament, cut into 8" lengths (for hangers)
Hand-sewing needle
Scissors
Measuring tape
Iron

1. Complete all cross stitch following instructions given.
2. Trim cross-stitch fabric to within 1" around perimeter of stitched design.
3. Fuse Wonder-Under™ to back side of stitched design, following manufacturer's instructions for fusing. Peel away paper backing and fuse felt to wrong side of stitched design. Trim close to edge of design around perimeter of ornament, following lines of design as a guide for cutting. Treat raw edges with Fray-Check™. Let dry. Apply a second coat of Fray Check™, if desired.
4. Thread needle with blending filament, stitch through top of ornament, and tie filament ends in a knot to form hanger.
5. Repeat for remaining ornaments.

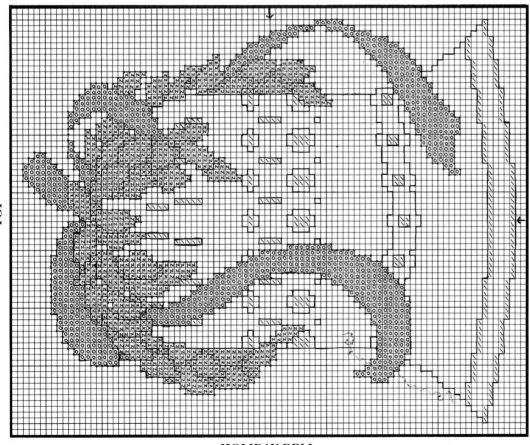

HOLIDAY BELL

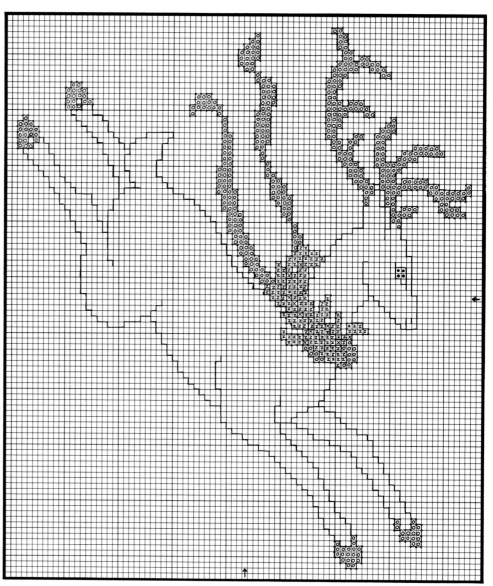

LEAPING REINDEER

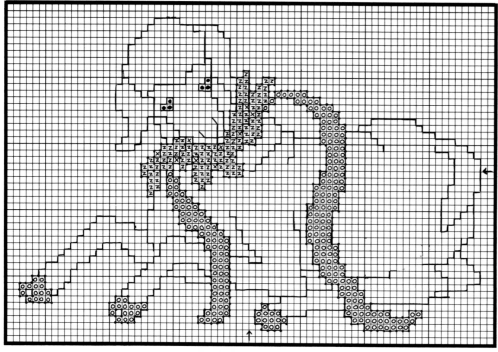

RESTING LAMB

28

PRANCING REINDEER

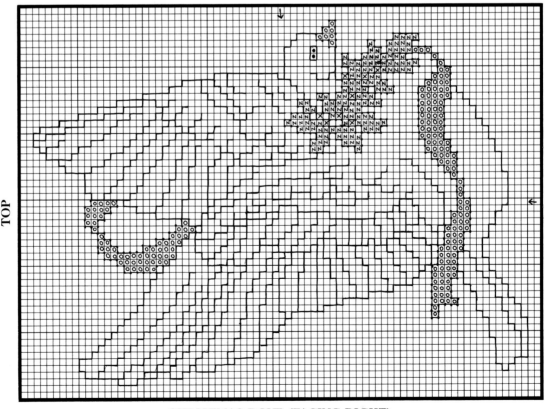

TOP

CHRISTMAS DOVE (FACING RIGHT)

POINSETTIA

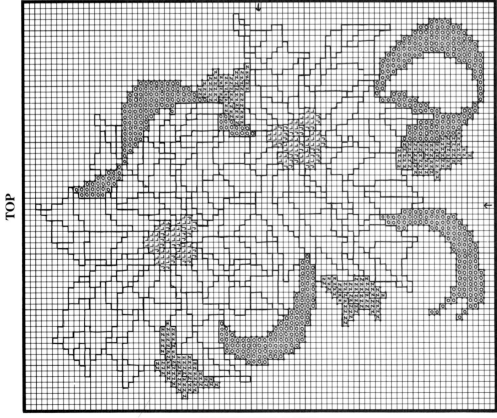

POINSETTIA DUET

TOP

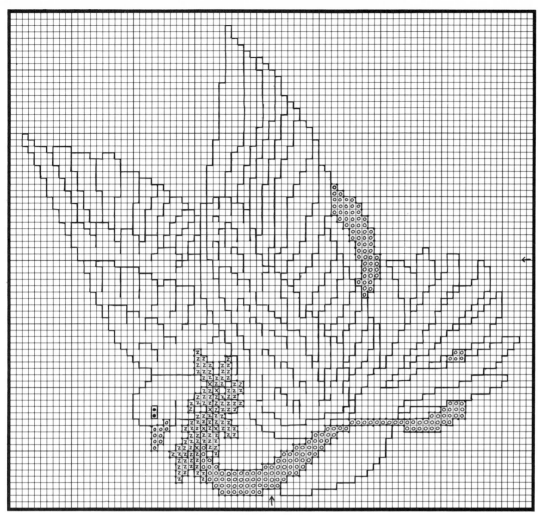

CHRISTMAS DOVE (FACING LEFT)

CHRISTMAS DOVE

31

SET A
FESTIVE TABLE

Here in America, we celebrate Christmas with a bounty of delectable edibles, from deliciously wholesome to scrumptiously sweet! Some of our fondest moments were those times spent preparing for the holidays with our mothers and grandmothers. Whether crafting decorations for use in our homes or finishing last-minute gifts, kneading the dough for home-made breads or garnishing frosted sugar cookies with colorful sprinkles, we still eagerly anticipate the season ahead and reminisce about those we have already celebrated. Because so many yuletide festivities center around taste treats and temptations, it is only natural that the table has become a focal point throughout this most joyous time of the year.

The Center of Attention

We have found over the years that while some holiday decorations, such as the evergreen tree, remain basically the same, other areas offer great possibilities for creating a new look each year. Our favorite "Christmas quick changes" are centerpieces, which can be used on an informal kitchen table for family dinners, on a more formal dining room table or buffet for special gatherings, or even atop a table in the foyer to welcome yuletide visitors.

Whether made using fresh greenery or assembled from inanimate materials, tabletop arrangements can be used to convey a multitude of decorating themes.

For those who decorate the day after Thanksgiving, opportunities abound for using more than one centerpiece on each table as the season progresses. Included on these pages are centerpieces which are fairly quick and easy to as-

semble, and which are constructed from readily available materials. You will probably be pleasantly surprised at the amount of usable supplies you will find on hand by simply checking the attic and your sewing basket before sitting down to make your shopping list. You may even have some of the live greenery you will need growing in your own backyard!

If you are searching for the perfect elegant centerpiece for your holiday table, try the trio of *White Net Trees*. Sprinkled with gold sequins and topped with gold metallic ribbon bows, this three-

some will add sparkle to any setting. For a decidedly different look, craft the trees in another color or mix and match colors for an unforgettable tabletop display.

For trouble-free decorating your visitors are certain to remember long after they've headed home, suspend doily snowflakes from the limbs of a bare-branched tree or create your own interesting look with light-weight ornaments of your choosing.

For more centerpiece crafting ideas, turn the page!

Opposite—Simple and tasteful, this trio of White Net Trees *will form a stylish arrangement when displayed with crystal candlesticks, golden star garland, and a blanket of "snow" underneath it all. Just be certain to place the candles and the trees far enough away from each other to prevent them from becoming a fire hazard. Instructions are on page 43.*

Above—A unique way to show off a special collection of ornaments is by tying them on a bare-branched tree. A collection of small crocheted doilies provides the decoration for this painted tree. Using fabric stiffener, we transformed inexpensive purchased doilies, available at most craft stores, into beautiful ornaments. Instructions for Doily Ornaments *are on page 43.*

Right—*The traditional fruit stack has long been a favorite. Though this centerpiece looks complicated, with our easy-to-follow instructions it can be made for use in your home, too. Instructions for Fruit Stack are on page 43.*

Below—*Remember the old plastic fruit in the attic? Use it to make "Antiqued" Fruit Centerpiece. Add lace scraps, paint, and brush with gold paint for a Victorian look. Embellish with silk greenery and pearl-colored beads for a tabletop focal point sure to win admiring looks from your guests. Instructions are on page 44.*

Above—*Canning jars that clutter the pantry shelf can be put to good use this Christmas. Arranged with flowers and greenery, the jars house small candles. The effect is wonderful, and the jars keep little hands from the candles. Instructions for Canning Jar Centerpiece are on page 44.*

Above—*The Candles And Holly centerpiece uses cuttings from bushes you may have in your yard to bring a bit of nature to your decorating scheme. Made with holly leaves, this table adornment can also be formed using evergreen sprigs to add a delightful fragrance to your home. Instructions are on page 44.*

36

SET A FESTIVE TABLE

Beautiful Beginnings

While busily making a collection of lovely centerpieces, be sure to set aside some time to stitch and sew table accessories for them as well.

Table coverings and linens can be used to set the mood for your yuletide party, whether your aim is cozy and casual or undeniably elegant.

Shown on this page, the simple *Patchwork Tablecloth* will come in handy for holiday parties as an over cloth and is the perfect size to cover a card table for holiday bridge. Sew the cloth as shown, in checkerboard fashion with traditional reds and greens, or select scraps of assorted Christmas print fabrics left in your sewing box and make your cloth with a colorful variation of fabrics. The results will be charming and your guests will be impressed.

***Above**—Constructed using the most basic of sewing techniques, this easy-to-complete* Patchwork Tablecloth *is ideal for a small table and can also be made to cover a larger surface by simply adding additional squares. Instructions are on page 44.*

The poinsettia, with its origins in Mexico and Latin America, has become synonymous with Christmas in many areas of the world. Used for decorating and often given as a gift, it is perhaps the most widely accepted floral symbol of Christmas in America.

Opposite, a variation on familiar seasonal colors features the beautiful poinsettia, stitched in shades of pink, on place mats for your dining table. Matching napkins are achieved by working single bows to correspond to the place mat bows and streamers.

On this page, the spectacular poinsettia is worked in traditional Christmas colors on fashionable wearing apparel. Adorned with this eye-catching flower, this comfy sweatshirt dress can go from shopping to home entertaining with ease. Touches of metallic threads

Opposite—The stunning poinsettia, worked in unexpected colors, forms breathtaking table linens for the holidays. Stitch enough pieces to use for a large, formal gathering or create two sets of these attractive linens to establish the tone for a romantic dinner for two.

Above left—Declare your love for Christmas in stitches worked atop comfortable wearing apparel that looks as good as it feels! A successful blend of the trendiness of modern times and the tradition of days gone by, the sweatshirt dress and poinsettia design are teamed up to make a first-rate fashion statement.

Left—Ideal for home decorating as well as for gift-giving, the table runner can be stitched to use alone or as an accent to matching place mats and napkins. Charts and color codes for Poinsettia Stitchery begin on page 46.

add special sparkle, and a single bow adorns one sleeve of the festive garment.

The versatile table runner, with showy poinsettias in opposite corners, matches the place mats and napkins. It can be used in the center of the dining room table, as well as atop a buffet or sideboard. Holiday entertaining takes on an enchanting air when you cleverly combine your stitchery and the filled punch bowl. Consider this pleasing presentation for a Christmas wedding reception or bridesmaids' luncheon.

A splendid mix of holiday-inspired stitchery and plaid fabric, woven with a hint of metallic thread, creates the charming *Bells-N-Bows Table Runner.* The bell and garland motif is repeated many times over to adorn the sides of this useful piece, and each bell is completed with a three-millimeter gold bead, tacked at the bottom. Easy to finish, this runner can be used

season after season for a beautiful table. If you choose, work the motif on place mats and finish them with matching plaid fabric. Hem plaid squares to form quick-to-complete napkins. Whether you make only the runner or fashion an entire collection of table linens with the bells and bows design, you're certain to garner praise from all your dinner guests during the holidays!

Quilting is truly an American art form and usually brings to mind handmade masterpieces featuring classic fan or star designs. Another form of quilting, called yo-yo quilting, is seen perhaps less often today but is an interesting needle craft that is a snap to learn and is a lot of fun, too! The first yo-yo quilting many of us remember was done by our grandmothers when we were young girls. We watched, fascinated, as Nana's skilled hands quickly pulled the little medallions of fabric into gathered circles that would become

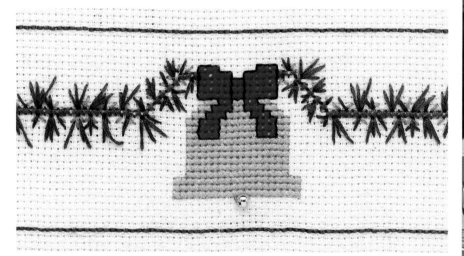

Above—Close-up of bell and garland motif shows detail. **Right**—*The* Bells-N-Bows Table Runner *works splendidly in a formal dining room. Finished with pleated plaid fabric, this finery makes a wonderful beginning for a classic holiday dinner setting. Chart is on page 45.*

beautiful bed covers. Those of us fortunate enough to inherit those wonderful warmers display them proudly in our homes today. Fast and affordable, this quilting technique is also versatile and is an excellent portable project. Use travel time while vacationing to start making your yo-yo circles and have them ready for assembling when you return home. In addition to making unique bed covers, yo-yo circles are fantastic for trimming table linens, clothing, and countless other items. Yo-yo-trimmed table linens are featured here. For a festive sweatshirt adorned with yo-yo circles, turn to page 118.

***Above**—Red and white mini-dot fabric place mats and a matching table runner trimmed with yo-yo circles spell a whimsical beginning for a holiday table. Instructions for* Yo-yo Creations *are on page 43.*

Yo-yo Creations

Materials:
3 yds. 44/45"-wide Christmas print fabric (for table runner and place mats)
1½ yds. 44/45"-wide complementary lining fabric (for table runner and place mats)
Purchased sweatshirt with ribbed neck band (medium)
¼ yd. 44/45"-wide complementary Christmas print fabric (for first chain on sweatshirt)
¼ yd. 44/45"-wide complementary Christmas print fabric (for second chain on sweatshirt)
Thread to match
Hand-sewing needle
Scissors
Sewing machine (optional)
Measuring tape
Iron

Note: Yardage given will make four place mats, one table runner, and yo-yo trim for one medium sweatshirt. These projects can also be made from non-holiday colors, which will make them ideal for use the whole year through.

1. Cut table runner and lining 9½" x 30". Place right sides together and stitch all four sides, leaving an opening for turning. Clip corners, turn, and press. Whipstitch opening closed and topstitch ¼" from edge.
2. Cut place mats and lining 13" x 17" and follow instructions given in #1.
3. Cut fourteen 3½" circles for each place mat. Cut forty-six circles for table runner. Stitch around each circle from wrong

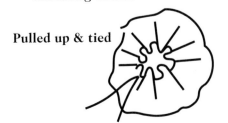

Gathering thread

Pulled up & tied

side of fabric, turning raw edge under ¼" (toward wrong side of fabric) as you go and leaving thread tails for forming yo-yo. Pull thread tails tight to form yo-yo, tie thread ends to secure, and clip close to knot.
4. For table runner, tack yo-yos together to form a chain. For place mats, tack seven yo-yos together for each end. Tack yo-yos around perimeter of table runner and to each end of place mats.
5. To trim sweatshirt, cut sixteen circles for inner chain (closest to band) and twenty-one circles for outer chain. Follow instructions for making yo-yos, tack together as for table runner and tack around sweatshirt, placing top edge of inner chain approximately ¾" from seam where neck band is joined to sweatshirt. Place outer chain directly underneath inner chain.

Doily Ornaments

Materials:
Purchased white crocheted doilies
Fabric stiffener
Large **rustproof** straight pins
Plastic wrap
Cardboard or corkboard
White thread, cut into 8" lengths (for hangers)
Measuring tape
Hand-sewing needle
Scissors

1. Cover cardboard with plastic wrap.
2. Saturate doily in fabric stiffener and squeeze out excess. Do not wring. Place doily on board and pin into shape. Let dry overnight.
3. Remove stiffened doily from board. Thread needle with white thread, stitch through hole in top of doily "arm," and tie a knot in thread ends to form hanger.

White Net Trees

Materials:
3 pieces white plastic foam (for tree bases): one with 2¼" diameter, two with 3" diameters
Three ⅜" dowel pins: one 8" long, one 12" long, one 18" long
4 yds. white nylon net
7½ yds. gold metallic ribbon (for bows)
10"-length 18- or 22-gauge wire for **each** tree
Measuring tape
Gold sequins
White paint
Tacky glue

Note: Materials listed will make three *White Net Trees*: one small, one medium, one large.

1. Paint dowel white and glue into plastic foam base.
2. Cut fabric into strips, beginning with the most narrow width for the size tree you are making and increasing the width of each strip by ½", until you reach the measurement of the widest strip needed for the tree you are making (as indicated below).

For small tree, cut two strips, each 1" wide. Then cut two strips, **each 1½" wide**, two strips, **each 2" wide**, and two strips, **each 2½" wide** (36-38" long strips; 8 strips total).

For medium tree, begin with two strips, **each 1" wide**, and end with two strips, **each 4" wide** (46-48" long strips; 14 strips total).

For large tree, begin with two strips, **each 1½" wide**, and end with two strips, **each 6" wide** (52" long strips; 20 strips total).
3. Run gathering thread along one long edge of strip. Gather. Overlap ends of strip, forming a circle to fit around dowel pin. Repeat for all strips and place on dowel with the widest strips on the bottom and the most narrow on the top.
4. Glue on sequins as desired.
5. Make bow, referring to "How-Tos For Making A Bow" on page 105, and glue to top of dowel. (Small bow requires 1½ yds., medium bow 2½ yds., and large bow 3½ yds.)

Note: Some of the centerpieces, such as the *Fruit Stack* and the *Candles And Holly*, are perishable. For best results, craft them as close as possible to the day you plan to use them.

Fruit Stack

Materials:
18" plastic foam cone
Large plate or platter
30 wooden skewers
12–14 apples
12–14 lemons
Whole pineapple
Cooking oil
Boxwood
Soft cloth
Ice pick

Note: Materials listed will make one *Fruit Stack*.

1. Set plastic foam cone on plate.

2. Polish apples and lemons, using small amount of cooking oil on soft cloth.
3. Spear fruit pieces with wooden skewers and attach fruit to cone, spacing evenly for balance.
4. Fill in empty spaces with boxwood.
5. Spear bottom center of pineapple with ice pick, insert skewer, and attach pineapple to top of cone.

Candles And Holly

Materials:
Flat dish
Floral oasis (to fit on dish)
Tesa® film (a tape-like substance that sticks in water, available at floral shops)
Fresh holly
Taper candles
4 yds. ribbon of your choice (for bows)
20 in. 18- **or** 22-gauge wire
Measuring tape
Wire cutters **or** utility scissors

Note: Materials listed will make one *Candles And Holly* centerpiece.

1. Center floral oasis on dish and adhere oasis to dish using Tesa® film. Wet oasis thoroughly.
2. Insert candles and holly into oasis, referring to photo on page 36 for placement.
3. Cut wire into two 10-inch lengths. Make two bows, using two yards of ribbon for **each** and referring to "How-Tos For Making A Bow" on page 105.
4. To complete arrangement, secure bows by inserting wire ends into oasis, referring to photo on page 36 for placement.
Note: Trim wire ends as needed to secure bows at a pleasing height.

Canning Jar Centerpiece

Materials:
3 canning jars, with lids
Wooden lazy Susan **or** tray of your choice
Assorted flowers and greenery
3 votive candles
1½ yds. white yarn, cut into 18" lengths
1½ yds. gold metallic cord, cut into 18" lengths

1. Remove flats from rings and screw rings onto jars.
2. Place one piece yarn and one piece metallic cord together, aligning ends. Tie in a bow under ring around top of jar. Repeat for remaining jars.
3. Place candles in jars.
4. Place jars in center of lazy Susan.

Arrange flowers and greenery around jars, as desired.

"Antiqued" Fruit Centerpiece

Materials:
Assorted plastic fruit
Silk evergreens
Silk greenery with pinecones
1"-thick 7½" x 4" piece plastic foam (for base)
Gesso acrylic undercoating
4 yds. ribbon of your choice
White acrylic paint
Gold spray paint   Gold oil paint
Paintbrushes; one small, one fine
Assorted flower motifs cut from lace
Floral tape   Floral wire
Wooden picks   Glue

Note: Materials listed will make **one** *"Antiqued" Fruit Centerpiece.*

1. Coat fruit with gesso.
2. Paint fruit white, using small paintbrush. Let dry.
3. Glue on flower motifs as desired.
4. Paint with a second coat of white, painting over flower motifs. Let dry.
5. Using fine brush and oil paint, "antique" fruit gold. Let dry.
6. To prepare fruit pieces for arranging, cut floral wire into pieces approximately eight to ten inches long. At one end of each piece of fruit, make two small holes (one in each side of fruit). Run wire in hole on one side, through hollow center, and out hole on other side. Pull wire through fruit until you have equal amounts of wire on both sides. Wrap wire ends to pick, securing with floral tape. (If one end of pick is blunt, and the other is sharp, wrap wire at blunt end, leaving sharp end for arranging fruit in plastic foam base.)
7. Arrange silk evergreens in plastic foam base, adding silk greenery, pinecones, and fruit, as desired.
8. Cut two 20" lengths floral wire for securing bows. Make two bows, using two yards of ribbon for each and referring to "How-Tos For Making A Bow" on page 105.
9. To complete arrangement, secure bows by inserting wire ends into plastic foam, referring to photo on page 36 for placement.
Note: Trim wire ends as needed to secure bows at a pleasing height.

Patchwork Tablecloth

Materials:
1¼ yds. 44/45"-wide green Christmas fabric of your choice

1¼ yds. 44/45"-wide red Christmas fabric of your choice
5½ yds. complementary lace of your choice
Thread to match fabric and lace
Measuring tape   Pinking shears
Scissors   Iron   Hand-sewing needle
Sewing machine (optional)

Note: Materials listed will make one *Patchwork Tablecloth.* We suggest using a permanent press fabric for this project for ease of care.

1. Cut forty-nine 8" squares (twenty-five green and twenty-four red).
2. Lay out squares in rows, alternating red and green squares.
Note: You will have seven rows of seven squares each. Begin four rows with green squares and three rows with red squares.
3. Stitch squares together to form rows, using a ½" seam allowance. Pink raw edges to prevent fraying. Press seams open.
4. Stitch rows together to form tablecloth, using a ½" seam allowance and matching seams (as if matching plaid) to align squares in a checkerboard fashion. Pink raw edges to prevent fraying and press seams open.
5. To finish, make a ¼" shirttail hem around perimeter of tablecloth. Attach lace around edge of tablecloth atop hem, mitering at corners.

Bells-N-Bows Table Runner

DMC	Kreinik Metallies	Color
V 937		avocado, med.
X 817		coral red, vy. dk. (two skeins)
– 783		gold
∕ 3345		hunter, dk. (two skeins)
ss 936		avocado, vy. dk.
ss 3347		yellow-green, med.
bs 310		black
bs	002C	gold cord

Fabric: 14-count white Aida from Charles Craft, Inc.
Stitch count: 308H x 840W
Design size:

11-count	28" x 76⅜"
14-count	22" x 60"
18-count	17⅛" x 46¾"
22-count	14" x 38¼"

Instructions: Cross stitch using three strands of floss. Backstitch using one strand of floss unless otherwise indicated. Straight stitch using two strands of floss.

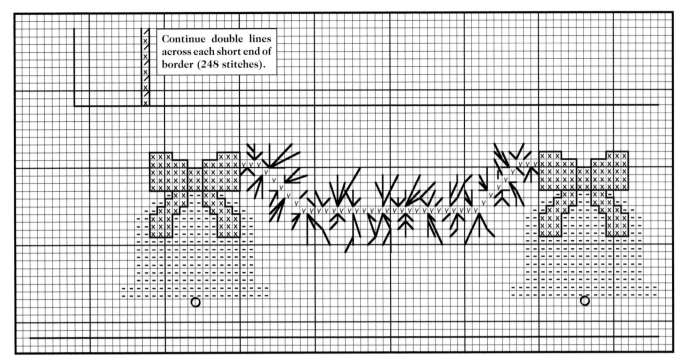

Continue double lines across each short end of border (248 stitches).

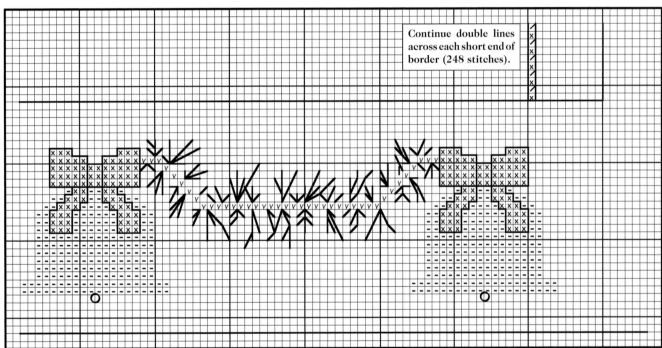

Continue double lines across each short end of border (248 stitches).

Center 15 bells on each long side. From backstitch to edge of design is 7 threads (½").

Backstitch (bs) instructions:

310	around bows
3345	border of design (two strands)
002C	trim of red and green at each end of runner

Straight stitch (ss) instructions:

3345	longest needles on bough
3347	alternate stitches on bough
936	alternate stitches on bough

Materials:

1¼ yds. 44/45"-wide plaid fabric with gold metallic thread (for pleated trim)

Thread to match plaid   Iron
2 yds. 44/45"-wide white fabric (for backing)
Thirty 3-mm gold beads   Scissors
Sewing machine   Measuring tape
Hand-sewing needle   Straight pins

Note: Materials listed will make one *Bells-N-Bows Table Runner.*

1. Complete all cross stitch following instructions given.

2. Cut plaid lengthwise into 6"-wide strips.

3. With right sides together, sew strips end to end to form a single long strip. With wrong sides together, fold strip in half lengthwise and press.

4. Pin pleats at 1½" intervals entire length of fabric. Baste along raw edge.

5. Pin pleated trim to right side of runner, placing raw edges together. Sew pleated trim to runner, using a ⅝" seam allowance and easing at corners.

6. Pin white backing fabric to runner with right sides together, making sure pleated trim lays flat so as not to catch it when sewing front and backing pieces together. Sew around runner, using a ⅝" seam allowance and leaving a 4" opening for turning. Trim seams, clip corners, turn right-side out, and slip stitch opening closed. Press.

Poinsettia Stitchery—
Table Linens

DMC	Kreinik Metallics	Color
V 605		cranberry, vy. lt.
‖ 604		cranberry, lt.
o 603		cranberry
• 602		cranberry, med.
− 504		blue-green, lt.
T 503		blue-green, med.
X 502		blue-green
∶ 827		blue, vy. lt.
+ 519		sky blue
∪ 518		Wedgwood, lt.
M 517		Wedgwood, med.
·ᛁ· 676		old gold, lt.
♡ 729		old gold, med.
bs	#5	gold, Japan Thread
bs	#5	silver, Japan Thread

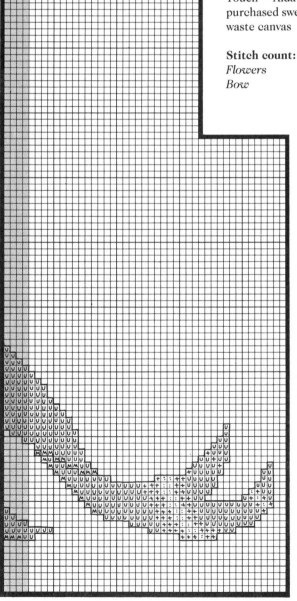

Shaded portion indicates overlap from previous page.

Sweatshirt Dress

DMC	Kreinik Metallics	Color
∪ 726		topaz, lt.
+ 725		topaz
∶ 783		gold
M 782		topaz, med.
• 816		garnet
o 304		red, med.
‖ 498		red, dk.
V 321		red
·ᛁ· 445		lemon, lt.
♡ 973		canary, bt.
X 700		green, bt.
T 701		green, lt.
− 702		kelly green
bs 444		lemon, dk.
bs	#8	silver, Japan Thread
bs	#8	gold, Japan Thread

Fabric: 14-count pink soufflé Soft Touch™ Aida from Charles Craft, Inc.; purchased sweatshirt dress and 10-count waste canvas

Stitch count:

Flowers	140H x 140W
Bow	42H x 43W

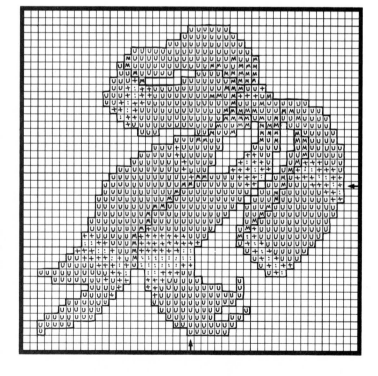

Design size:

Flowers

10-count	14" x 14"
14-count	10" x 10"

Bow

10-count	4⅛" x 4⅜"
14-count	3" x 3⅛"

Instructions: Cross stitch using three strands of floss. Backstitch using two strands of floss unless otherwise indicated. Standard size place mat is 13" x 18". Standard size napkin is 15" x 15". Size of runner will be determined by size of table and whether runner is placed horizontally or vertically on table. When making accessory table linens from scratch, cut fabric approximately 2" larger on all sides than finished size desired. *Sweatshirt Dress:* Referring to photograph on page 38, position design, using waste canvas.

Backstitch (bs) instructions:

Table Linens
— #5 gold, Japan Thread (one strand)
•••• #5 silver, Japan Thread (two strands)
ıııı 729 (center of flower)

Sweatshirt Dress
— #8 gold, Japan Thread (one strand)
•••• #8 silver, Japan Thread (two strands)
ıııı 444 (center of flower)

DECORATE WITH NATURALS

You may have joined the ranks of environmentally conscious recyclers or you may be fascinated with the idea of creating seasonal decorating items the way our ancestors did—with the abundance of materials provided by nature. Either way, we think you will love this assortment of almost-all-natural crafts. From prickly pinecones to gorgeous dried flowers, you can harvest a bounty of natural items for making pieces you will be proud to display in your home. You can also enjoy crafting for others who share your preference for a holiday season reminiscent of those from the simpler days of our forefathers. These projects will provide many hours of crafting fun as well as great exercise as you comb the outdoors for the materials needed to construct them!

own home year after year or give them as gifts to close friends and relatives. You can also change the colors of the sequins and paints used, if you like, to customize the trees to match a particular decor or to create an entirely different look for the elegant trio.

When your time is short but you still want to give a gift that's from the heart, try the quick-to-complete *Straw Candle Ring.* It is sure to be a hit with all those folks on your gift list who prefer seasonal decorating with just a whisper of rural charm.

For simple-to-make kindling with a decorative twist, create *Pinecone Fire Starters.* They will put an end to that messy stack of newspapers and make it possible for you to start a cozy fire with ease. Make plenty to store in a basket set on the hearth for all your holiday festivities. Fun to craft, these pieces will be a thoughtful gift for neighbors who have a fireplace in their home!

Above and right—Acorn Cap Trees *add an unexpected twist to yuletide decorating. To make an elegant statement, use the* White Acorn Cap Tree *and the* Gold Acorn Cap Tree, *above. For a less-formal look, display the* Natural Acorn Cap Tree, *right. Instructions are on page 58.*

53

DECORATE
WITH NATURALS

Topiary Trees

Topiary trees are becoming more and more popular as wonderful home-decorating pieces that are displayed both during the holidays and throughout the year. Whether made from natural materials or crafters' silk, they make interesting accents and splendid gifts!

Those who love flowers can enjoy the appeal of beautiful blossoms all year long with decorative pieces which feature dried blooms. Add a special touch to a foyer or hallway with a breathtaking trio of Victorian-inspired *Pastel Flower Trees*. Fashioned with baby's breath, miniature roses, and assorted dried flowers, these pieces will lend a welcoming air to your seasonal festivities.

Left—Eye-catching and aromatic, the Dried Flower Tree *features colors which can be used in a variety of decorating schemes when the holidays are over. Instructions begin on page 58.*
Right—A trio of Dusty Miller Trees *will work splendidly for an all-white Christmas. Instructions are on page 59. For information on preserving flowers, turn the page.*

Using an array of topiary trees is a great way to spread a bit of the Christmas season throughout the house. Just before the weather turns frosty, pick dusty miller from your yard or from a neighbor's yard with her permission, and gather goldenrod from country roadsides to craft some of the topiary trees pictured here. The colors and materials used for most of these trees will also make them perfect display pieces long after the holiday glow has faded.

Opposite—Inspired by the ornateness of the Victorian era, the Pastel Flower Trees *will impart a feeling of romanticism in your holiday decorating. Instructions are on page 59. For information on preserving flowers, turn the page.*

Left—The Carnation Tree *is crafted with silk carnations and evergreen to form a decoration that features traditional holiday colors. Instructions are on page 59.* *Right—The* Goldenrod Tree *uses this colorful autumn-blooming plant in a showy presentation that forms a most interesting decorating piece. Instructions are on page 59.*

How To Preserve Flowers

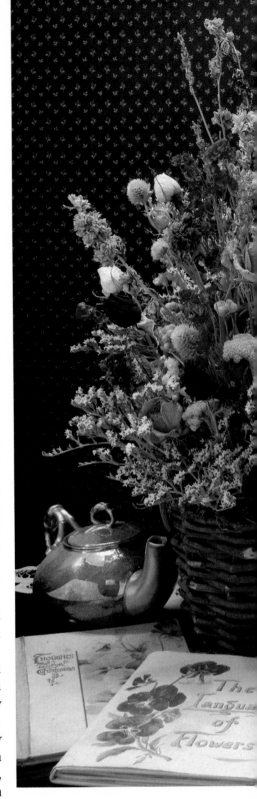

Drying flowers is one way to bring the natural beauty of the outdoors into your home.

Generally, flowers selected for drying should be cut just before they come into full bloom. Since drying involves a great deal of shrinkage, plan accordingly the quantity you will dry.

There are numerous methods for drying flowers, but perhaps the two simplest are the air-drying method of hanging and the surrounding and covering method.

The hanging method works well for most flowers. This method involves suspending flowers upside down, either individually or in bunches. When hanging flowers in small bunches, ensure adequate air circulation and prevent distortion by making sure the blossoms do not touch each other. For best results, hang flowers in a warm, dark, dry place, such as an attic or a closet, and leave them to dry. The darkness is essential as sunlight will fade the colors; and the area must be free from high levels of moisture, which will hinder the appearance of the dried blooms.

The surrounding and covering method works well for flowers with large blooms, such as chrysanthemums, which would become drastically distorted if hung. This procedure involves the use of a chemical drying agent, such as silica gel. To use this method, surround the flowers to be dried with the product and cover them in a manner so that the gel lends support between petals. This keeps the shape of the flower head. Note that when this method is used, the blooms must be placed in an airtight container. Other products, such as a meal and borax mixture or crushed volcanic rock, may be used as drying agents, but silica gel tends to yield the best results, drying flowers thoroughly but allowing them to retain their color and form better than other agents. Although silica gel may seem costly, it is a one-time investment because it can be used over and over when properly stored and cared for according to the manufacturer's directions.

Drying time depends on the moisture content of the flowers, the medium used, and the temperature and humidity. A bloom can take from two days to five weeks to dry.

For making potpourri, you can use petals that break off as you arrange dried flowers or you can dry petals specifically for this purpose.

There are a number of ways to dry petals, including placing them on newspapers, drying them in the oven, or using drying racks. Drying on racks tends to yield the best results; and when this method is used, the racks must be placed away from strong light and in an area with good air circulation. Window screens, placed on bricks or concrete blocks, work perfectly as drying racks and can be stacked one foot apart.

Blossoms chosen for drying for use in potpourri should be just opened, at the peak of their bloom. Pick flowers late in the morning when there are no traces of dew remaining on them but before the sun is high. Snip a few leaves from the stems at the same time to add variety in both color and aroma.

Gently pull the petals from the blossoms and place on a drying

rack along with the leaves, being sure to spread them out so that they are only one petal deep. Drying time may take several days for the petals and leaves to dry to the right degree, which is comparable to a flake of cereal. Stir the mixture several times throughout the drying process.

To help preserve the aroma, add one teaspoon orrisroot, available in drug and health food stores, to one pint of dried petals and leaves. You can also add fragrance with oils, obtainable in scent shops, department stores, craft stores, and other retail establishments.

By drying blooms from nature's bounty, you can keep the aromas of seasons past and the vivid splashes of color displayed against a country hillside during the spring long after the weather has turned cold. For more information about drying and preserving fresh flowers, contact your local library.

57

Pinecone Tree

Materials:
33"-tall tomato cage (available at nurseries)
Assortment of pinecones
1 roll 24-gauge wire (you will have wire left over)
1 large ball 3-ply jute twine
Glue gun

Note: Materials listed will make one *Pinecone Tree.*

1. Turn tomato cage upside down and wire prongs together to form a cone shape. Turn cage right-side up.
2. Beginning at top, wrap twine vertically around wire rings of cage, spacing twine wraps approximately ½" apart as you go. Repeat around cage horizontally.
3. Referring to photo on page 51, wire pinecones as desired onto exposed metal. When metal is completely covered, fill in remaining areas, gluing additional pinecones to twine and covering tree completely with pinecones.

Acorn Cap Trees

Note: For these projects, a combined materials list and instructions are given. Those items appearing at the end of the materials list, without individual tree specification, are used for all trees. Specific instructions for individual trees are given in each note in the instructions.

Materials:
15"-tall plastic foam cone (for *Natural Acorn Cap Tree*)
1 pkg. bronze sequins (for *Natural Acorn Cap Tree*)
Design Master® color tool spray paint: Glossy Wood Tone (for *Natural Acorn Cap Tree*)
12"-tall plastic foam cone (for *Gold Acorn Cap Tree*)
1 pkg. red sequins (for *Gold Acorn Cap Tree*)
Design Master® color tool spray paint: Brilliant Gold (for *Gold Acorn Cap Tree*)
20"-tall plastic foam cone (for *White Acorn Cap Tree*)
Three 200-ct. pkgs. green sequins (for *White Acorn Cap Tree*)
Four 150-ct. pkgs. pearl beads (for *White Acorn Cap Tree*)
White fast-drying spray paint (for *White Acorn Cap Tree*)
Small acorn caps
Craft glue
Tacky glue
Paste stick
Needle **or** toothpick

Note: Materials listed will make one *Natural Acorn Cap Tree,* one *Gold Acorn Cap Tree,* and one *White Acorn Cap Tree.*

1. Spray plastic foam cones with designated color, following manufacturer's directions. Let dry.
Note: Do not spray cone for white acorn cap tree.
2. Using paste stick, apply tacky glue to back of acorn cap and press into cone, beginning at top, working down, and covering tree completely. Let glue dry.
3. Spray *Gold Acorn Cap Tree* again, and spray *White Acorn Cap Tree* a first time. Let dry. Do not spray *Natural Acorn Cap Tree.*
4. Insert tip of glue bottle into each acorn cap and apply a small amount of glue. Insert a sequin in each acorn cap. Let dry.
Hint: Dip end of needle or toothpick into glue to pick up sequins.
Note: On *White Acorn Cap Tree* only, use paste stick to apply a small amount of tacky glue in center of each sequin. Add a pearl bead in center of each sequin. Let dry.

Pinecone Fire Starters

Materials:
Red crayons, or other color of your choice
2 lbs. candle wax   Waxed paper
Pie plate   Cupcake liners
Muffin tins
6" candlewick (for **each** pinecone)
Small- to medium-sized pinecones
Glitter
Kitchen tongs
Double boiler

1. In double boiler, bring water to very slow boil.
2. Put wax in top of double boiler and melt.
3. While wax is melting, put cupcake liners in muffin tins and waxed paper on pie plate. Open glitter for easy accessibility. Tie candlewick around bottom of each cone.
4. Using tongs, dip one pinecone at a time in melted wax. Place on pie plate and sprinkle immediately with glitter.
5. Add crayons to remaining wax to achieve desired color.
6. Carefully pour colored wax into cupcake liners and set one pinecone in each.

Straw Candle Ring

Materials:
10" straw wreath
Four ¼"-thick wooden trees, each approximately 3½"-4" tall
2 yds. green paper cord
8"-long ⅛"-diameter wooden skewer
Green paint   Craft glue
Oil lamp **or** large candle and globe
Drill with 3/16" bit   Utility scissors

Note: Materials listed will make one *Straw Candle Ring.* Wooden cutouts are available at most craft stores. For variety, you may wish to use snowmen, reindeer, Santas, or other holiday motifs. If the cutouts you choose are of a different thickness than those listed above, be sure to take the difference into account when calculating the size of wooden skewer and drill bit needed, as skewer diameter must be less than thickness of cutout.

1. In the center bottom of base of each tree, bore a hole approximately ¼"-⅜" deep. Cut skewer into 2"-long pieces and glue into holes in bases of trees. Paint trees green. Let dry.
2. Untwist paper cord. Cut six 1"-wide strips, each two yards long. Wrap one strip around wreath, then wrap a second strip in opposite direction. Use remaining strips to make bows, referring to "How-Tos For Making A Bow" on page 105 and securing bow centers with paper cord. Glue bows onto wreath, spacing evenly.
3. Insert trees into wreath between bows.
4. Use oil lamp **or** large candle and globe in center.

Dried Flower Tree

Materials:
Assorted dried flowers
Purple statice
Spanish moss
Potpourri (optional)
18" stick **or** dowel
6" plastic foam ball
Large container
Piece of plastic foam (to fit in container)
5 yds. 2"-wide ribbon of your choice
10"-length pliable wire
Gold spray paint
Marbles **or** small stones
Florist's adhesive
Utility scissors
Ice pick
Glue gun

Note: Materials listed will make one *Dried Flower Tree.*

1. Spray plastic foam ball gold. Let dry.
2. Cut plastic foam piece (other plastic foam) to fit container. Use florist's adhesive to attach plastic foam piece in

container. Insert stick in plastic foam piece, taking care to center stick in container. Fill remainder of container with marbles or small stones to provide balance for completed project. Cover with Spanish moss.

3. Insert end of stick approximately 2" into plastic foam ball.

4. Carefully punch holes in plastic foam ball, using ice pick. Cut dried flowers and statice into assorted lengths. Cover ball completely with statice and dried flowers, gluing stems into holes. Fill in bare spots by gluing dried flower heads to statice.

5. Use ribbon to make bow, referring to "How-Tos For Making A Bow" on page 105. Using wire, attach bow to base of tree.

6. Sprinkle potpourri around base of tree, if desired.

Dusty Miller Trees

Materials:
Dried dusty miller
33"-long ⅜"-diameter dowel
Three 3" plastic foam balls
Small pieces of plastic foam
Gray acrylic paint
6 yds. ¾"-1"-wide silver ribbon
Three 4" clay pots
Plaster of paris
3 silver grape clusters
30" pliable wire, cut into 10" lengths
Spanish moss   Paintbrush
Glue gun   Utility scissors
Ice pick   Scissors

Note: Materials listed will make three *Dusty Miller Trees.*

1. Cut dowel into three pieces: one 9", one 11", and one 13" long.

2. Paint clay pots and dowels pale gray. Let dry.

3. Insert a dowel approximately one inch into each plastic foam ball.

4. Place a piece of plastic foam in each pot and insert other end of each dowel, taking care to center dowels in pots. Mix plaster of paris according to manufacturer's instructions and pour around plastic foam piece and dowel. Fill pot about ¾ full. Hold dowel until plaster of paris begins to set.

5. Carefully punch holes in plastic foam ball, using ice pick. Break dusty miller into 3"- to 4"-long pieces and glue into holes. Use leaves to fill in bare spots.

6. Glue ribbon around top of each pot. Divide remaining ribbon into three equal lengths and make bows, referring to "How-Tos For Making A Bow" on page 105. Using wire, attach a bow to base of each tree.

7. Fill remainder of pot with Spanish moss and dusty miller. Glue on grape clusters and bows.

Goldenrod Tree

Materials:
Dried goldenrod
15"-tall plastic foam cone
Gold spray paint
Hair spray
Glue gun

Note: Materials listed will make one *Goldenrod Tree.*

1. Spray plastic foam tree gold.

2. Glue goldenrod spikes over entire tree.

3. Beginning at bottom of tree, glue on individual spikes, one at a time, to form branches.

4. Spray tree with three to four coats of hair spray.

Carnation Tree

Materials:
3 dozen red silk carnations
Silk evergreen
German statice
16"-long ¼"-diameter dowel
4" plastic foam ball
Small piece plastic foam
2 yds. ¾"-1"-wide red velvet ribbon
10"-length pliable wire
4" clay pot
Gold spray paint
Green acrylic paint
Plaster of paris
Utility scissors
Glue gun
Ice pick

Note: Materials listed will make one *Carnation Tree.*

1. Paint clay pot and dowel green. Let dry.

2. Spray paint plastic foam ball gold. Let dry.

3. Place small piece of plastic foam in pot and insert one end of dowel, taking care to center dowel in pot. Mix plaster of paris according to manufacturer's instructions. Pour around plastic foam and dowel. Fill pot about ¾ full. Hold dowel until plaster of paris begins to set.

4. Insert other end of dowel approximately one inch into plastic foam ball.

5. Carefully punch holes in plastic foam ball, using ice pick. Cut greenery, carnations, and statice into 3"- to 4"-long pieces and glue into holes.

6. Glue ribbon around top of each pot. Use remaining ribbon to make bow, referring to "How-Tos For Making A Bow" on page 105.

7. Fill remainder of pot with statice. Glue on bow.

Pastel Flower Trees

Materials:
Three plastic foam trees: 12", 10", 8" tall
6 yds. ¼"-wide mauve satin ribbon (3 yds. for 12" tree, 1½ yds. **each** for 10" and 8" trees)
Glue gun
Scissors
Utility scissors
Baby's breath
Globe amaranths: pink, white
Strawflowers: mauve, cream
Mauve glittered baby's breath

Note: Materials listed will make three *Pastel Flower Trees.*

1. Glue amaranths and strawflowers on tree and fill in spaces with baby's breath, referring to photo on page 54.

2. Cut mauve glittered baby's breath 2" long and glue on as desired.

3. For treetop, cut several 3"-4"-long pieces of ribbon and glue to top of tree. Arrange remaining ribbon in loops, gluing to treetop as you go. Glue several pieces of glittered baby's breath into loops.

4. Repeat for remaining trees.

Pinecone And Nut Wreath

Materials:
15" straw wreath (for large wreath)
6" grapevine wreath (for small candle ring)
20"-length pliable wire (for hanger)
Small pinecones
Assorted, unshelled nuts: Brazil nuts, almonds, hazelnuts, acorns, walnuts, hickory nuts, peanuts
Peach pits
Spray varnish
Glue gun

Note: Materials listed will make one large *Pinecone And Nut Wreath* and one *Miniature Pinecone And Nut Candle Ring.*

1. Wrap wire around what will be the large wreath, make a wire loop for hanger, and twist wire ends together to secure.

2. Glue nuts on inside of each wreath first.

3. Glue nuts, pinecones, and peach pits around outside of each wreath and then fill in top portion.

4. Spray with varnish. Let dry.

WELCOME HOLIDAY GUESTS

Yuletide entertaining provides wonderful opportunities for families and friends to gather and share the enchantment of Christmastime! If the annual event is at your home this year, you'll want to be certain your guests feel welcome—and what better way to invite them into your abode than with a lighted walkway that leads to the front door, decorated and ready for the holidays. Whether your residence conveys an undisputed elegance or a casual country flair, you can greet your visitors in superb style this Christmas with an assortment of craft projects beckoning your callers inside to enjoy a festive celebration!

WELCOME
HOLIDAY GUESTS

Luminarias

Mark the way to your holiday parties with our adaptation of *luminarias*. The Latin American custom calls for small lighted candles to be placed in paper bags and used to light walkways and streets during the holiday season. This tradition, which originated in Mexico and spread to many cities in the American Southwest, is great to adopt whether you live in Boise or Boston or somewhere in between! Your guests will feel your warm holiday wishes when they step out of their cars to find a welcoming curbside glow leading them straight to your front door. They will never guess you have recycled small metal cans in assembling these impressive outdoor ornaments.

For an unforgettable Christmas Eve service, get together with a group from your church several weeks ahead of time and share favorite holiday tales as you craft enough *luminarias* to line the sidewalks leading to the front door of the church. Put them outside the night of the service and let them set the mood.

A note of caution: Because *luminarias* are made with paper, they are flammable. Cans in the bases are filled with sand for stability, but we suggest using your *luminarias* only on still, windless nights. Use caution when lighting and decorating with these welcoming pieces and handle them with care.

Left and right—Using this trio of designs, make enough luminarias *to light the path to your front door. Send a holiday welcome to visitors with these popular seasonal motifs—Holly Luminaria, Candle Luminaria, and City Luminaria. Instructions begin on page 68.*

Making An Entrance

Decorating doors throughout your home—from the main entrance to the kitchen—is an excellent way to welcome guests and to show your fondness for the season. From beautifully elegant to sweet and simple country, these decorations will enhance most any door in your home. Below left, a *Topiary Tree* boasts traditional seasonal colors with bright red craft apples and green leaves. The trio of golden *Pinecone Bells*, below right, can grace a variety of entryways in absolutely breathtaking style. For those who may be worried about whether Santa Claus will fit through the chimney, the larger-than-life *Noel Stocking*, strategically placed on the front door, is a guarantee that its owner won't be forgotten on Christmas morn!

Those who prefer to celebrate Christmas with a rural atmosphere will enjoy using the *Clothespin Ring*, pictured on the following page, to convey the message that the folks who live here are lovers of country through and through. By combining everyday items with a few craft pieces and by following our easy instructions, you can create a wreath that's sure to be a conversation starter, especially when you hang it on your laundry room door!

For quick and easy kitchen decorating, craft the appealing

Red craft apples and plastic green boxwood picks have been combined to make this pleasing Topiary Tree, a fantastic seasonal decoration which can also be displayed the whole year through. Instructions are on page 67.

This golden trio of bells forms an appealing door embellishment. Ideal for use at Christmastime, this piece will lend a touch of sophistication to your decorating. Instructions for Pinecone Bells are on page 67.

Cross stitch and sewing have been paired to create this charming oversized Noel Stocking, *fabulous for yuletide decorating and for holding a multitude of holiday goodies! Instructions begin on page 70.*

Strawberry Wreath, below left. The red mini-dot fabric is perfect for creating the cloth berries and is usually available in fabric stores year-round. Make the berries while snowbound during the winter or while on vacation during the summer, and they'll be ready to place on a silk evergreen wreath in time for the holidays. Add a matching fabric bow and display your completed project in a favorite spot. Of course, the completed wreath, although it boasts traditional holiday colors, could also be displayed all year if it matches your home's decor. If you are especially fond of strawberries or have included them in your kitchen decor, fashion enough of these fabric berries to fill a basket in your kitchen the whole year through!

Above left—*The delightful* Clothespin Ring *will be perfect for decking the halls or, in this case, the doors for the season ahead. Ideal for use where the decor is decidedly country, this wreath will be great for displaying on the laundry room door! Instructions are on page 67.*

Left—*This colorful display features red mini-dot fabric strawberries and a matching bow glued to a silk evergreen wreath. Instructions for* Strawberry Wreath *begin on page 67.*

Topiary Tree

Materials:
6" plastic foam ball
Cinnamon stick **or** wooden dowel
Basket of your choice
Plastic foam to fill basket
48 boxwood picks
12 to 14 medium craft apples
Small craft apples (optional)
18- **or** 22-gauge wire (for hangers)
Large knife
Glue gun
Moss

Note: Materials listed will make one *Topiary Tree*. For tree "trunk," we used a cinnamon stick. However, this is extremely fragile; and for more support, you may wish to use a wooden dowel or other similar material, surrounded by several cinnamon sticks.

1. Cut plastic foam ball in half, using large knife.
2. Cut a piece of plastic foam to fit in basket and glue in place.
3. To make hanger for basket, insert one end of wire through bottom of basket. Bring wire over top of basket and join ends on back side of basket. Twist the ends together to form a hanger.
4. To make hanger for top of tree, insert one end of wire through middle of ball. Bring it up across what will be the top and join it to the other end on back side of ball, twisting them together to form a hanger.
5. Carefully insert one end of cinnamon stick into ball opposite wire hanger and other end into plastic foam piece in basket.
6. Cover ball and plastic foam in basket with moss, gluing as you go. Hang on wall and insert boxwood picks, covering ball and plastic foam in basket.
7. Glue on medium craft apples and fill in with small craft apples, if desired.

Clothespin Ring

Materials:
14" wooden hoop
16" wooden hoop (optional)
88 clothespins
8 small clothespins (available at craft stores)
2 wooden cutouts (available at craft stores)
15 yds. natural jute twine
Acrylic paint: red
Paintbrush
Spray varnish
Wood glue

Tape measure
Utility scissors

Note: Materials listed will make one *Clothespin Ring*. For this wreath, we used one wooden hoop. If you plan to use the wreath on an outside door, we suggest using two hoops for added stability.

1. Glue clothespins around perimeter of hoop, placing clasp end of each toward center.
Note: If using two hoops, place them on a flat surface and center 14" hoop inside 16" hoop. Glue clothespins around perimeter of hoops, placing clasp ends toward center and making sure springs rest in the area between the two hoops.
2. Paint small clothespins and edges of cutouts red. Thin a portion of paint with water and paint a thin wash over entire cutout, leaving more color around outside edges. Let dry. Paint on lettering with unthinned paint. Let dry.
3. Varnish wreath and cutouts. Let dry.
4. Tie short piece of twine to top of wreath, making a loop for hanging.
5. Cut 22"-long piece of twine and weave through holes in cutouts. Tie twine ends to wreath. Glue a small clothespin at top corners of each cutout.
6. With remaining twine, make bow for top of wreath by looping twine back and forth, gluing as you go. Wrap end of twine around center of bow once and glue bow to wreath, centering over hanging loop. Cut one loop from each side of bow in half to make four tails. Glue one small clothespin to each tail.

Pinecone Bells

Materials:
3 bells (plastic foam **or** papier-mâché)
6 yds. antique-gold paper cord
Pinecones
Gold spray paint
18- **or** 22-gauge wire (for hangers and securing center of bow)
Wire cutters   Glue gun

Note: Materials listed will make one set of *Pinecone Bells*.

1. To make hanger for each bell, insert one end of wire through top of bell. Bring wire across top of bell and join it to other end of wire, twisting ends together to form hanger.
2. Remove burs from pinecones, using wire cutters or by breaking off with fingers.
3. Beginning at bottom, glue a row of burs around each bell. Add one row at a time, overlapping each row and covering

bells from bottom to top.
4. Spray bells with gold paint. Let dry.
5. Untwist cord. Cut three different lengths of your choice to hang bells. Run a piece of cord through each hanger. Glue.
6. Make a bow from remainder of untwisted cord, securing in center with wire and referring to "How-Tos For Making A Bow" on page 105.
7. Use wire to attach bells to back of bow.

Strawberry Wreath

Materials:
18" silk evergreen wreath
⅓ yd. 44/45"-wide red/white mini-dot fabric
One 9" x 12" piece green felt
12"-long green pipe cleaner (for wreath hanger)
Thread: red, green
Polyester filling
Sewing machine
Measuring tape
Hand-sewing needle
Scissors
Glue gun
Iron

Note: Materials listed will make one *Strawberry Wreath*.

1. Cut a 4"-wide, 44"-long strip from red/white mini-dot fabric. Fold with right sides together along lengthwise edge and stitch all three sides ⅛" in from edge, leaving a 2" opening for turning. Turn and press. Baste opening closed. Tie to form a bow. Set aside.
2. Enlarge strawberry and cap patterns (see page 68) as indicated. Place cap pattern on green felt and cut fourteen pieces. Set aside. Place strawberry pattern on remaining mini-dot fabric and cut fourteen pieces. Fold right sides of fabric together and stitch along straight sides, using a ⅛" seam allowance. Turn right-side out and stuff firmly with polyester filling. Hand baste at top of strawberry ⅛" in from edge of fabric, pull basting thread to gather along top, and tie thread ends to secure. Tack cap to strawberries at top and at each point.
3. Wrap one end of pipe cleaner around wire form of wreath at what will be top and twist pipe cleaner to secure. Form a small loop for hanging with remainder of pipe cleaner and twist to secure.
4. Glue strawberries to wreath, spacing evenly, or as desired, and attach bow at bottom of wreath.

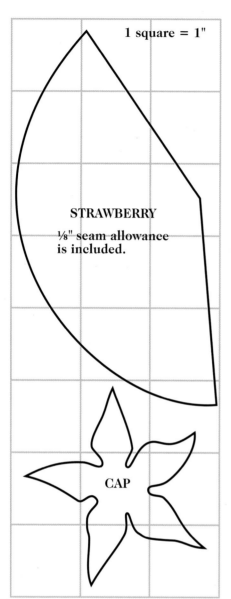

1 square = 1"

STRAWBERRY

⅛" seam allowance
is included.

CAP

Luminarias

Materials:

Two 12" x 18" sheets translucent drawing
paper (model made with Manila paper)
12½ oz. empty tuna can, washed, with
label removed
Votive candle in fire-safe container
Tracing wheel **or** scrap of plastic
needlepoint canvas
Non-flammable glue stick
Craft knife
Paper punch
Paper-cutting scissors
Sand
Large sharp needle (optional)
Long fireplace matches (for lighting)

Note: Materials listed will make one
Luminaria.

1. Enlarge patterns as indicated. Cut
first sheet of paper 13⅓" x 12".
Note: If you choose a different kind of
can, be sure it has at least a 4" diameter.
Using a smaller can will result in a fire
hazard. Measure the circumference of
the can you use and add ¾" for overlap at
back.
2. For *City Luminaria,* trace city and
star shape on second sheet of paper. Cut
out. Glue onto back side of first sheet
of paper. For *Candle Luminaria,* trace
candle, flame, and candle holder on second sheet of paper. Cut out. Cut out
center of flame where *X* appears. Glue
onto back side of first sheet of paper. For
Holly Luminaria, trace holly on back of
second sheet of paper. Cut out leaves and
thin stem. Punch out seven berries from
scrap paper, using paper punch. Glue
berries to cut-out design. Glue cut-out
design (whole page) to back of first sheet
of paper. For all luminarias, use only **non-
flammable** glue. Be sure to place designs
above top of can, or they will not show.
For *City* and *Candle Luminarias,* pierce
paper to make rays of light, using a
dressmaker's tracing wheel or a scrap of
plastic canvas to make perfectly spaced
holes. If you wish to make holes larger,
place paper atop a medium-soft surface
and punch through first set of holes
using a large, sharp needle.
3. To assemble each luminaria, glue paper into a tall cylinder around can, placing cut and glued pattern on inside of
cylinder. Put sand in can and add votive
candle in fire-safe container. Light candle
carefully, using long fireplace matches
and being careful not to ignite paper
walls of luminaria.
4. Place luminarias in safe locations only.
Keep luminarias well out of the reach of
children. **Do not** leave luminarias unat-
tended while candles are lit.

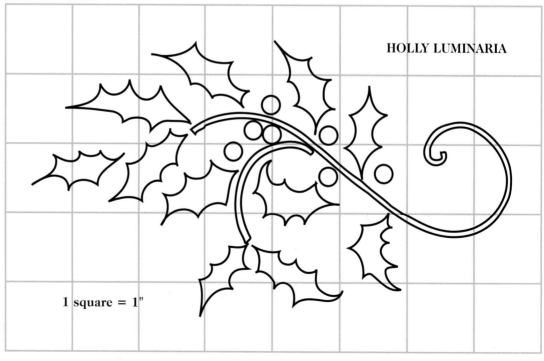

HOLLY LUMINARIA

1 square = 1"

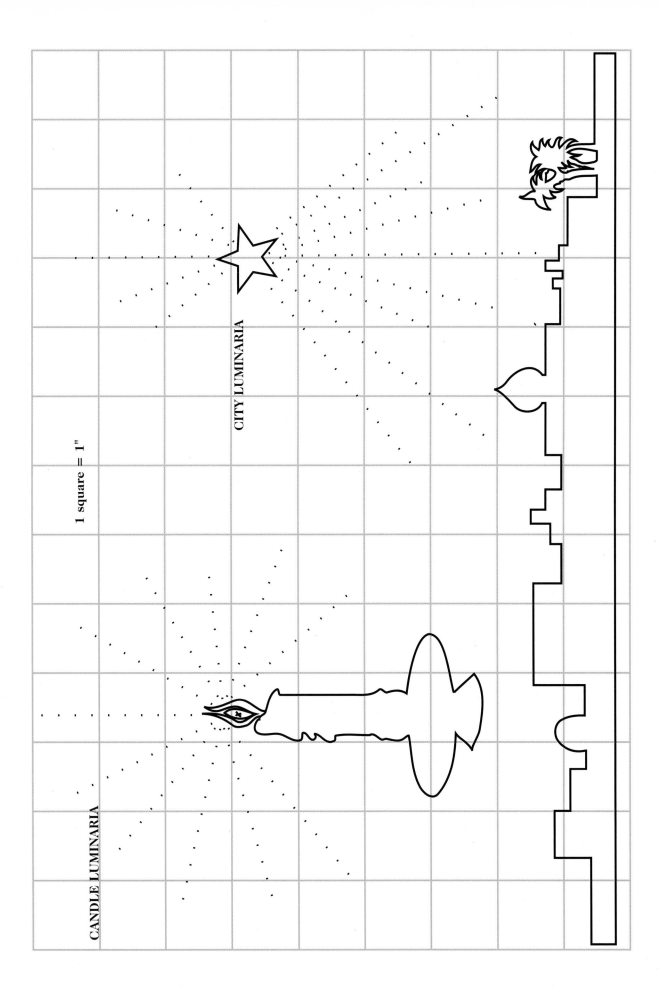

CITY LUMINARIA

CANDLE LUMINARIA

1 square = 1"

69

Noel Stocking

DMC	Color
M 355	terra cotta, dk.
S 356	terra cotta, med.
· white	white
V 932	antique blue, lt.
+ 931	antique blue, med.
*⌐ white	white
⌊ 319	pistachio green, vy. dk.
■ 890	pistachio green, ultra dk.
● 699	Christmas green
W 700	Christmas green, bt.
6 701	Christmas green, lt.
╱ 725	topaz
− 726	topaz, lt.
L 321	Christmas red
o 304	Christmas red, med.
3 434	brown, lt.
X 435	brown, vy. lt.
╵ 436	tan
╲ 437	tan, lt.
bs 939	navy blue, vy. dk.
bs 712	cream

Fabric: 14-count cream Aida from Zweigart®
Note: Cut 7" x 24" piece 14-count cream Aida for cuff.

Stitch count: 71H x 164W
Design size:

11-count	6½" x 14⅞"
14-count	5⅛" x 11¾"
18-count	4" x 9⅛"
22-count	3¼" x 7½"

Instructions: Cross stitch using two strands of floss. Backstitch using one strand of floss. Make French knots using two strands of floss, wrapping floss around needle twice. When two colors are bracketed together, use one strand of each.

Backstitch (bs) instructions: Backstitch in order listed.

321	four small candy canes in border
700	bow ties on two large gingerbread men
939	gingerbread men, smiles on two large gingerbread men
712	bands on arms and legs of small gingerbread men
321	red swirl on either side of *Noel*
890	windows on houses and inside doors
321	stripes on large candy canes
939	remainder of backstitching

French knot instructions:

939	eyes on gingerbread men
321	noses on small gingerbread men
701	buttons on small gingerbread men
321	doorknobs on left and right houses, center of crosses on middle and right houses, holly berries

Materials:
26"-length cream lace trim
⅝ yd. prequilted fabric of your choice (for stocking)
8"-length ½"-wide complementary ribbon (for hanger)
Sewing machine (optional)
Disappearing ink marking pen
Measuring tape
Thread   Scissors   Iron

Note: Materials listed will make one *Noel Stocking.*

1. Complete all cross stitch following instructions given.
2. Enlarge stocking pattern as indicated. Fold pre-quilted fabric in half with right sides together and place pattern atop fabric. Trace around pattern and cut out.
3. Stitch around edges of stocking, placing right sides of fabric together, using a ⅝" seam allowance and leaving top of stocking open. Trim seams. Set aside.
4. To make cuff, place cross-stitch fabric with right sides together, align raw edges, and stitch seam, using a ⅜" seam allowance. Press.
5. Beginning at seam, hand-stitch or machine-stitch lace to lower edge of cuff with right sides together, overlapping lace at ends. Fold lace down, turning raw edge of cuff under, and press lace and cuff.
6. Fold ribbon in half to form hanging loop and baste hanging loop at top of stocking on back side. With right side of cuff to wrong side of stocking, place cuff at top of stocking so that stitched design is to the front. Stitch cuff to stocking, using a ⅝" seam allowance. Turn stocking right-side out, fold cuff down, and press.

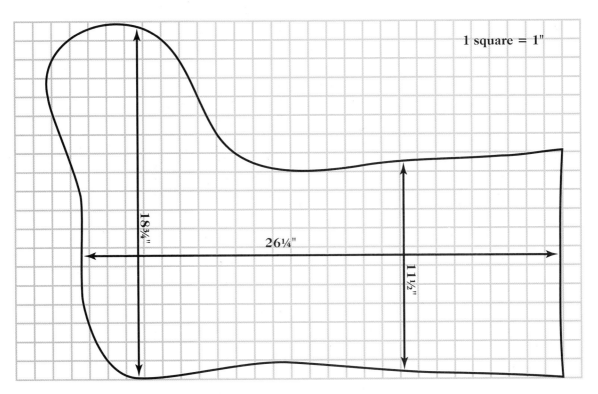

1 square = 1"

18¾"

26¼"

11½"

MAKE CHRISTMAS TREASURES

Beautiful needlework, inspired by the magic of Christmas, pulls at our heartstrings. Home-decorating treasures, created with this old form of art, are held forever dear by those who cherish fine handwork. Most needleworkers we know love to create quick-to-complete stitchery. However, their favorite works, created with needle in hand, are those more significant endeavors. These projects are often begun with fervor, put aside temporarily in order to finish other smaller ones, and then picked up again to be completed in time to decorate for the season with unforgettable style.

Needle Art To Cherish

If you have always wanted to master special holiday projects yet you find you don't have the time and energy to complete them once the annual Christmas rush begins, plan ahead. Get started early on those items you know will require significant amounts of your time and ambition. Think of your planning and organizing as a "countdown to Christmas," and get set for many enjoyable hours of stitching.

Whether your passion is for counted cross stitch or quilting, the only form of needle art native to the United States of America, you are certain to enjoy the many pleasurable hours you spend creating these handmade masterpieces that will deck your halls in splendor throughout the yuletide season.

On the facing page, a traditional *Fan Quilt*, constructed with patterned fabrics in an assortment of festive seasonal colors and motifs, makes an unforgettable decorating statement. Of course part of the charm of handmade quilts is that no two are exactly alike; but by following the patterns and instructions for this magnificent quilt, you can make a similar piece you will be proud to display in your home during the holidays and the whole year through. Choose calicoes in Christmassy reds and greens or, for a new, unexpected twist, select eye-catching fabrics in favorite colors of your choice to make a quilted wonder. You might even construct this beauty using scraps left over from other projects. For added fun, invite your daughters or granddaughters to join you for a "quilting bee" and delight in the laughter and love as you fashion this cozy warmer together.

Left—If your holidays call for a touch of whimsy, this lovable reindeer will fill the bill. Certain to gain a giggle from the young and a smile from the young-at-heart, this charming design, finished as a wall hanging, will be right at home above a mantel and will work equally well hung in a welcoming foyer. Chart for Happy Holly Deer is on page 83.

Above—*Featuring a traditional quilt design, this colorful Fan Quilt was created with holiday-inspired fabrics that make this warmer a striking Christmas classic. Completed with a variety of quilting patterns, it is certain to become a treasured family heirloom for many generations to come. Instructions begin on page 80.*

Above—*Mark in stitchery a special little one's very first Christmas. His mother will adore it today, and he will grow to appreciate it in the years ahead. Finish your work as a photo frame and place his Christmas picture inside. Chart for* Baby's First Christmas *begins on page 86.*

Above and left—Golden-winged angels herald the season in this specially matted Christmas sampler, titled Peace On Earth. For versatility, the bands could also be worked as borders on a variety of decorative pieces, and selected motifs, stitched individually, will make lovely ornaments. Chart begins on page 88.

For those who have fireplaces in their homes, holiday mantel decorations are an absolute must. Whether you prefer decorations that lend a decidedly formal touch, such as the *Holly And Ivy Mantel Cloth* on this page, or those which convey an undisputed whimsical flair, like the *Happy Holly Deer* wall hanging on page 74, these designs are certain to tickle your fancy.

We think your children will take a liking to the fun-loving character on the *Happy Holly Deer* wall hanging. They will giggle with delight at this reindeer wearing a large green bow tied around his neck, ornaments dangling from his antlers, and an expression which makes him downright endearing.

The *Holly And Ivy Mantel Cloth*, displayed across an exquisite white mantel, may remind you of the fancy cloths which hung above the fireplaces at your grandparents' homes. We think you'll like the idea of incorporating a touch of the past in your home. We requested that our designer create a modern-day mantel cloth featuring cross-stitched ivy, holly leaves, and berries, worked with rich floss colors. The design is repeated across the length of the linen cloth, which has been fringed and knotted to give this piece an elegant finish.

You can mark a special event for your little one or for a precious grandchild with *Baby's First Christmas*, pictured on page 76. Train cars provide an ideal spot for the date, and playroom favorites have been stitched together to send along happy holiday wishes. Finished as a photo frame, the cheery design features cuddly teddy bears, friendly snowmen, and lots of stitched presents and toys for good little girls and boys!

Welcome the holidays with stitchery that is certain to become an annual favorite. The *Peace On Earth* sampler, pictured on page 77, combines cross-stitched symbols of the season to form a tree-shaped Christmas sampler, the focal point of this foyer vignette. For quick-stitch variety, work only the star, facing angels, and *Noel* for use in the window of a wooden candle rack.

With each stitch you take on your "countdown to Christmas," you're sure to be touched by the art of the needle and the spirit of this giving season.

Above—Familiar holly and ivy lend an elegant feeling to yuletide decorating when worked across a length of linen to form a striking mantel cloth. Complete the stitching and enjoy watching a Christmas classic or two on television as you fringe and knot your Holly And Ivy Mantel Cloth. *Chart begins on page 84.*

Fan Quilt

Note: Please read all instructions carefully before beginning. Use a ¼" seam allowance unless otherwise indicated.
Block: 12" x 12"
Quilt Size: 80" x 80"

Materials:
4 yds. 44/45"-wide muslin fabric (for 12½" blocks and perimeter triangles A)
2½ yds. 44/45"-wide red- and-green print fabrics (for fan blades B and crescents C)
1½ yds. 44/45"-wide red mini-check fabric (for inner sashing)
3½ yds. 44/45"-wide green solid fabric (for sashing, border, and binding)
6 yds. 44/45"-wide complementary backing fabric, pieced to fit 84" x 84"
84" x 84" piece batting
Cardboard or plastic template material
Pencil
Thread to match fabrics
Hand-sewing needle
Scissors
Sewing machine (optional)
Straight pins
Ruler   Iron   Quilting needle

1. Trace pieces B and C onto template material. Cut out. Using a ruler, draw templates: one 9½" square, one 12½" square (piece A), and one 17½" square. Cut out.
2. Using templates, cut 13 (12½"-square) background blocks A from muslin. Cut 78 fan blades B and 13 crescents C from assorted Christmas print fabrics, adding ¼" seam allowances.
3. Hand- or machine-piece 6 fan blades together, referring to photo on page 75 for placement. Add crescent (piece C), and then appliqué fan to background block A. Repeat to make 13 blocks total.
4. Cut sashing as follows:
 72 (1¼" x 12½") strips from red mini-check fabric;
 36 (3" x 12½") pieces from green solid fabric;
 12 (4½") squares from

QUILT ASSEMBLY DIAGRAM

green solid fabric (for squares D);
 12 (4½") triangles from green solid fabric (for ½ squares E);
 42 (1¼" x 6½") strips from red mini-check fabric (for Xs on pieces D and E).
5. Make sashing bands by sewing a mini-check strip to each side of one green strip. Repeat to make a total of 36 sashing bands.
6. Join one red-and-green sashing unit (from #5) to top of each fan block. Join one red-and-green sashing unit to the bottom of each of 5 of the fan blocks.
7. Make X (D) and ½-X (E) squares by turning under ¼" seam allowance on red mini-check strips and appliquéing to green X (D) and ½-X (E) squares as shown in photo.
Note: Take care when making the ½ -X (E) square to appliqué the inner seam only and place the outer edge of the red even with the green.
8. Following Quilt Assembly Diagram, make 6 side sashes from ½-X (E) squares, sashes, and X (D) squares.
9. Cut 2 (9½") squares from muslin fabric. Cut these in half diagonally to form the 4 corner triangles F.
10. Cut 2 (17½") squares from muslin fabric. Cut these in fourths diagonally to form

the 8 perimeter triangles G.
11. Following Quilt Assembly Diagram, arrange fan blocks, sashing bands, and outer triangles in diagonal rows. Join rows.
12. For green outer border, cut and piece 4"-wide green solid fabric to fit outer measurement of quilt. The 4 lengths should each be approximately 90" long. Stitch outer border pieces to the 4 sides of the quilt and miter corners.
13. Layer backing fabric right-side down, batting, and completed quilt top right-side up on a large, flat surface. Pin and baste through all layers.
14. Quilt as desired, perhaps in the ditch around the fans, and add filler designs in the background and on the borders, referring to photo on page 75 for placement.
15. To make binding, cut green solid fabric in 2½"-wide strips and piece strips together to form a 340"-long strip of binding. Fold binding in half lengthwise with wrong sides together and pin around perimeter of quilt front, aligning raw edges. Stitch binding to quilt, using a ¼" seam allowance. Turn binding to back of quilt and blind stitch in place.
16. To hang your quilt for display, add a sleeve for a dowel. Sign and date your quilt in permanent ink on back.

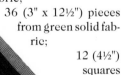

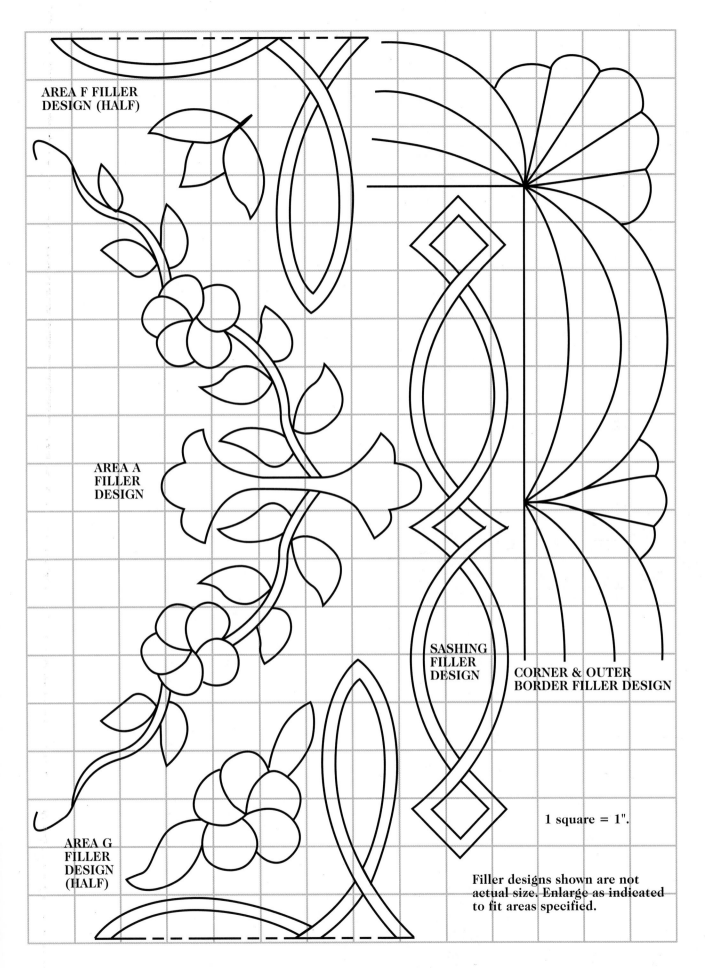

AREA F FILLER
DESIGN (HALF)

AREA A
FILLER
DESIGN

SASHING
FILLER
DESIGN

CORNER & OUTER
BORDER FILLER DESIGN

1 square = 1".

AREA G
FILLER
DESIGN
(HALF)

Filler designs shown are not
actual size. Enlarge as indicated
to fit areas specified.

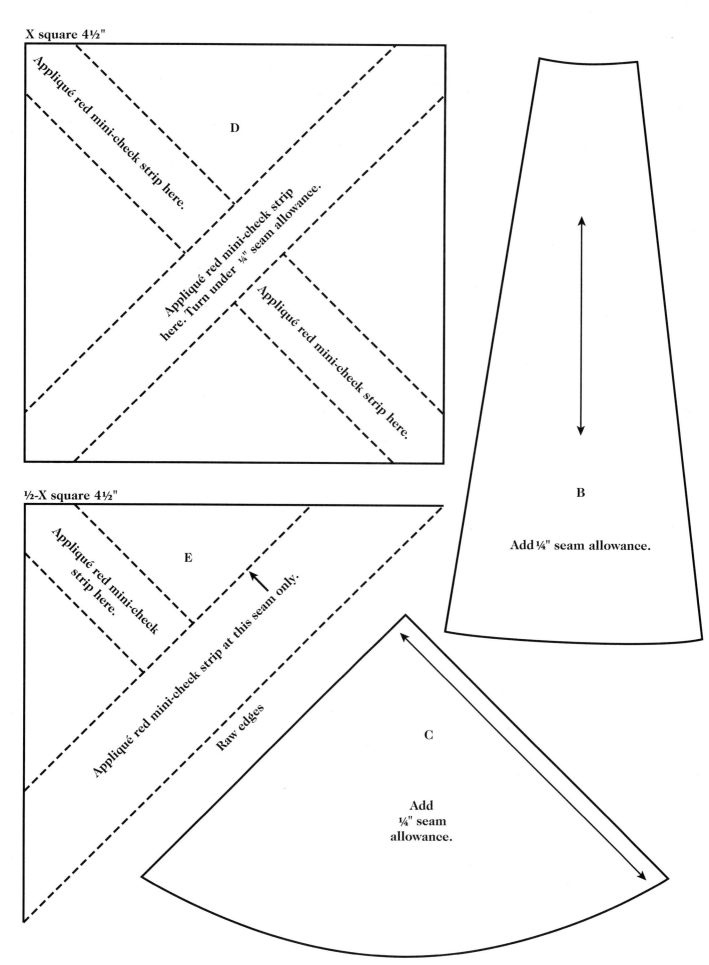

X square 4½"

D

Appliqué red mini-check strip here.

Appliqué red mini-check strip here. Turn under ¼" seam allowance.

Appliqué red mini-check strip here.

½-X square 4½"

E

Appliqué red mini-check strip here.

Appliqué red mini-check strip at this seam only.

Raw edges

B

Add ¼" seam allowance.

C

Add
¼" seam
allowance.

Happy Holly Deer

DMC	Color
L ecru	ecru
X 435	brown, vy. lt.
\ 436	tan
• 3371	black-brown
Z 304	red, med.
C 699	green
З 3024	brown-gray, vy. lt.
∧ 321	red
- white	white
e 437	tan, lt.
o 775	baby blue, lt.
/ 701	green, lt.

Fabric: 6-count cream Aida from Zweigart®
Stitch count: 129H x 88W
Design size:

6-count	21½" x 14⅝"
10-count	13" x 9"
14-count	9¼" x 6¼"
18-count	7⅛" x 4⅞"

Instructions: Cross stitch using six strands of floss. Backstitch using three strands of floss. Make French knots for gingerbread man's eyes and buttons using three strands 3371, wrapping floss around needle twice.

Backstitch instructions:
— 3371
ᴧᴧ 304

Happy Holly Deer

Note: Please read all instructions carefully before beginning. Approximate finished size for wall hanging is 34" x 28½" on 6-count cream Aida. Because this cloth will stretch a considerable amount as you work with it, you may wish to use an alternate stitch count (suggestions on page 83) if finishing as a wall hanging to help prevent the front from sagging on the finished project.

Materials:
1⅛ yds. 44"/45"-wide calico **or** other fabric of your choice (for borders)
30" x 39" piece muslin (for backing)
Thread to match fabric **and** muslin
28"-long dowel **or** yardstick (for hanging)
Disappearing ink fabric marking pen
Straight pins
Sewing machine
Measuring tape
Hand-sewing needle
Scissors
Iron

1. Complete all cross stitch following instructions given.
2. Cut calico border pieces as follows: bottom border, 30" x 4¾"; top border 30" x 7½"; side borders 35½" x 4½" **each**.
3. Find placement for calico border pieces by counting the squares in the cloth of the stitched front, instead of by measuring, to ensure straight, even lines. Beginning at bottom of stitched design, count down 36 squares (approximately 5") from lowest point of hooves. Mark fabric at this point with disappearing ink fabric marking pen. At top, count up 36 squares from highest point of antlers and mark. On each side, count out 36 squares from widest point of antlers and mark. Make several marks along all four sides of design to use as guides for border placement, following "track" of fabric. Transfer markings to back side of stitched piece and trace rectangular shape following markings, being careful to follow "track" of fabric.
4. To assemble front, pin side borders along markings with right sides together, using a ¾" seam allowance. Pin from wrong side of stitched piece so as not to sew over pins. Machine-stitch from wrong side, being careful to follow marked lines. Place top and bottom borders along markings on stitched front with right sides together, using a ¾" seam allowance. Pin as for side borders and stitch. Press.
5. Atop a flat surface with right sides together, place muslin over assembled front aligning at bottom and smoothing pieces to lay flat. Leave excess muslin, if

any, at top of design. Pin. Stitch together at bottom and sides, leaving top open for turning. Trim seams, clip corners, and turn right-side out. Press.
6. At top, trim any excess muslin even with top edge of calico. Stitch calico and muslin together close to top edge, joining the two pieces as one. Narrowly turn edge under twice and hem to finish raw edge. To make casing for hanger, fold single piece to back of wall hanging, making front of band 3" wide. Press top edge and pin to hold securely. Fold loose edge under, using original stitching line for top border as a guide. Pin and whipstitch loose edge to backing, leaving ends open.
Note: If you wish to machine-stitch, be sure to pin from front side and then stitch in the ditch.
7. Remove pins and slide dowel or yardstick through casing to hang.

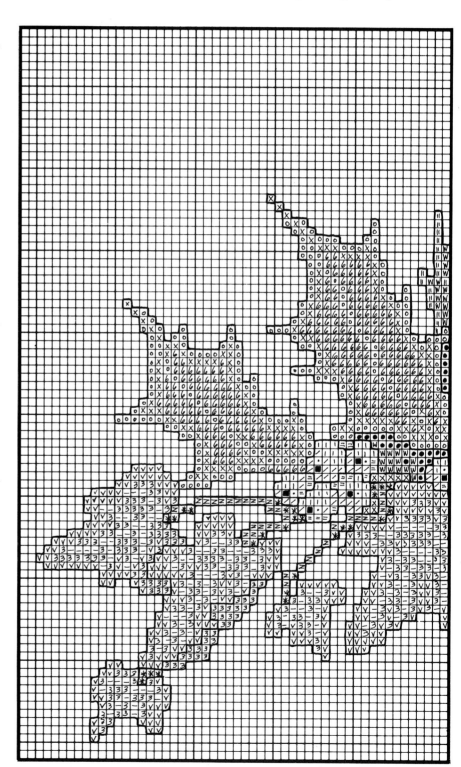

Holly And Ivy Mantel Cloth

DMC	Color
3 319	pistachio, vy. dk.
V 367	pistachio, dk.
- 368	pistachio, lt.
● 934	avocado-black
W 935	avocado, dk.
‖ 3011	khaki, dk.
6 469	avocado
X 470	avocado, lt.

o 3013	khaki, lt.
Z 611	drab brown, dk.
✳ 610	drab brown, vy. dk.
⏐ 304	red, med.
∕ 815	garnet, med.
= 814	garnet, dk.
■ 3371	black-brown
· 353	peach flesh

Fabric: 27-count off white linen from Norden Crafts

Stitch count: 85H x 130W
Design size:

11-count	7¾" x 11⅞"
14-count	6⅛" x 9¼"
18-count	4¾" x 7¼"
27-count	6¼" x 9¾"

Instructions: Cross stitch over two threads using two strands of floss. Backstitch using one strand 3371. Design is repeated three times, leaving seven inches between each design.

Shaded portion indicates overlap from previous page.

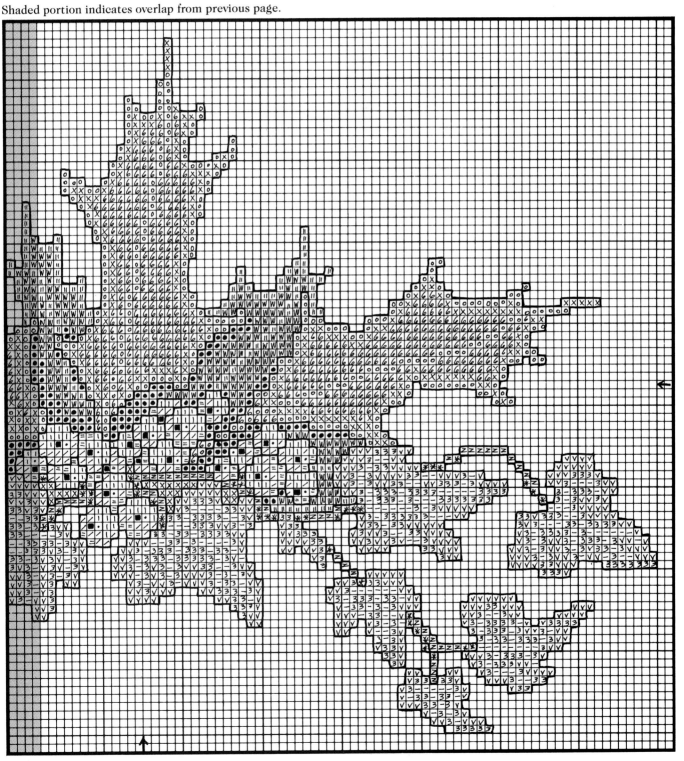

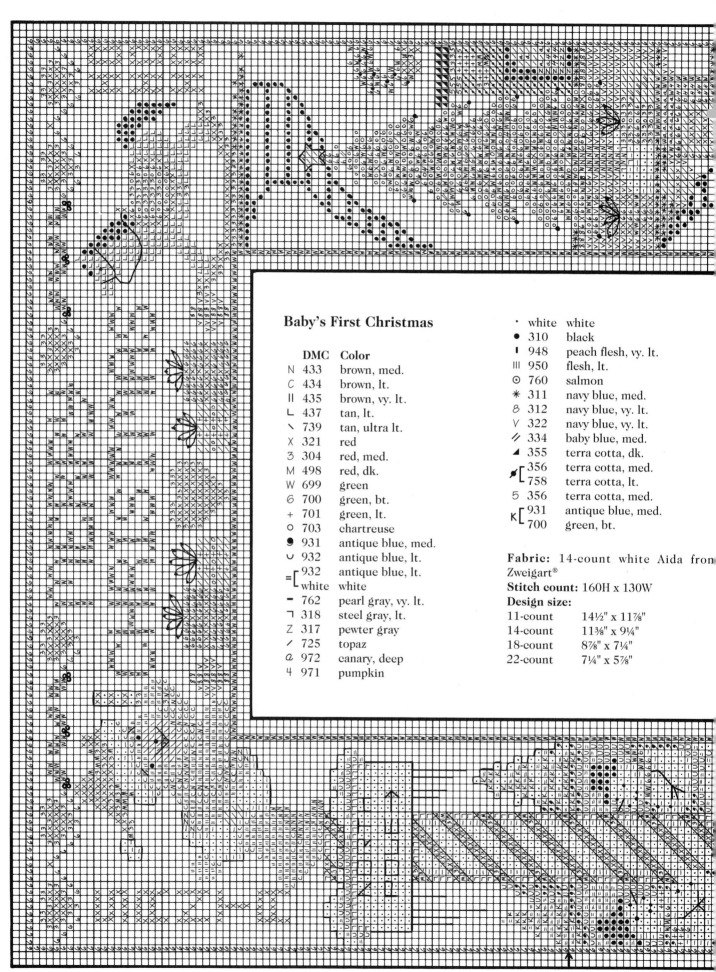

Baby's First Christmas

	DMC	Color
N	433	brown, med.
C	434	brown, lt.
II	435	brown, vy. lt.
L	437	tan, lt.
\	739	tan, ultra lt.
X	321	red
3	304	red, med.
M	498	red, dk.
W	699	green
6	700	green, bt.
+	701	green, lt.
o	703	chartreuse
9	931	antique blue, med.
U	932	antique blue, lt.
= [	932	antique blue, lt.
	white	white
−	762	pearl gray, vy. lt.
⌐	318	steel gray, lt.
Z	317	pewter gray
╱	725	topaz
a	972	canary, deep
4	971	pumpkin

	DMC	Color
·	white	white
●	310	black
I	948	peach flesh, vy. lt.
III	950	flesh, lt.
⊙	760	salmon
✳	311	navy blue, med.
8	312	navy blue, vy. lt.
V	322	navy blue, vy. lt.
╱╱	334	baby blue, med.
◢	355	terra cotta, dk.
✗ [	356	terra cotta, med.
	758	terra cotta, lt.
5	356	terra cotta, med.
K [	931	antique blue, med.
	700	green, bt.

Fabric: 14-count white Aida from Zweigart®
Stitch count: 160H x 130W
Design size:

11-count	14½" x 11⅞"
14-count	11⅜" x 9¼"
18-count	8⅞" x 7¼"
22-count	7¼" x 5⅞"

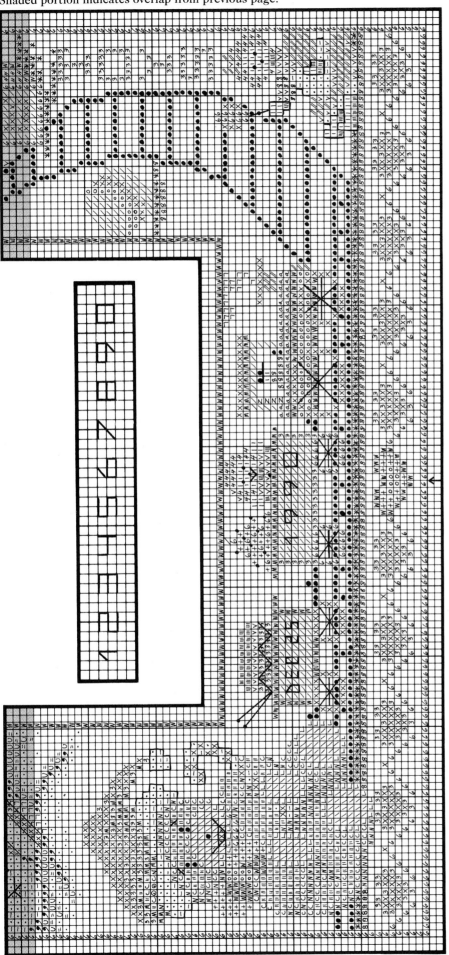

Instructions: Cross stitch using two strands of floss. Backstitch using one strand of floss unless otherwise indicated. Make French knots using two strands of floss, wrapping floss around needle twice. Make straight stitches and lazy daisy stitches using one strand of floss. When two colors are bracketed together, use one strand of each.

Backstitch instructions:

321	date on train, both dolls' mouths
700	rocking horse's bridle
310	eyebrows and mouth on both teddy bears, hat brim on train engineer
739	lines on drum
304	*North Pole* sign
971	snowmen's carrot noses
433	snowmen's twig arms
699	year on train
762	Santa hat, diaper

Straightstitch instructions:

932	icicles on sign
321	spokes on red wheels
699	spokes on green wheels
435	drumsticks
700	lollipop handle in doll's hand

Lazy daisy instructions:

700	bows on packages

French knot instructions:

321	holly berries (○), berries on Christmas trees and wreath
435	tips of drumsticks
760	dolls' noses
322	dolls' eyes
310	snowmen's eyes, mouths, and buttons; baby teddy bear's nose, rocking horse's eye

Finishing for photo frame: Purchase sticky board and easel back from local frame shop. Cut out center of sticky board and center of fabric for turning under, being careful not to clip too close to edge of border. (See illustration.) Trim outside edge, leaving enough fabric for turning under. Glue back to sticky board.

Note: Stitch on 14-count fabric to fit 5" x 7" photo.

Peace On Earth

DMC	Kreinik Metallics	Color
⊙ 355		terra cotta, dk.
∕ 677		old gold, vy. lt.
= 676		old gold, lt.
V 729		old gold, med.
2 680		old gold, dk.
W 433		brown, med.
● 801		coffee brown, dk.
− white		white
‖ 762		pearl gray, vy. lt.
✳ 3345		hunter green, dk.
M 895		Christmas green, dk.
3 347		salmon, dk.
X 3328		salmon, med.
＼ 760		salmon
· 754		peach flesh, lt.
6 930		antique blue, dk.
0 931		antique blue, med.
L 932		antique blue, lt.
+ 318		steel gray, lt.
⌐ 677		old gold, vy. lt.
⌊ 729		old gold, med.
ss	002HL-BF	gold, hi lustre

Fabric: 25-count white Lugana® from Zweigart® for *Noel*, 30-count unbleached linen from Norden Crafts for *Peace on Earth*

Stitch count: *Peace On Earth* 160H x 180W

Design size: *Peace On Earth*

18-count	8⅞" x 10"
22-count	7¼" x 8⅛"
25-count	12⅞" x 14½"
30-count	10⅝" x 12"

Instructions: Cross stitch over two threads using two strands of floss. Backstitch using one strand of floss unless otherwise indicated. Straight stitch using two strands of floss. Make French knots using two stands of floss, wrapping floss around needle twice. **Note:** Angels in second piece are stitched from chart. Letters for *Noel* were taken from verse and centered between angels using 680. To personalize, use alphabet to stitch your initials in corner wreaths. When two colors are bracketed together, use one strand of each.

Backstitch instructions:

347	bows on wreaths at top
680	eyes on angels
318	horns (two strands)
930	windowpanes
3328	bow on door wreath

French knots instructions:

3328	garland below poinsettia
676	center of each poinsettia in lower border (placed over cross stitch)
347	holly, bows at top, berries on initial wreaths

Straightstitch (ss) instructions:

002HL-BF	stars

Shaded portion indicates overlap from previous page.

CREATE QUICK GIFTS

Whether you plan months in advance for the holiday season or find yourself running out of stitching and crafting time before you reach the last name on your gift list, these quick and easy projects will make wonderful presents! If your penchant is for stitchery, you'll love the assortment of quick-stitch ideas included in this chapter, from designs for a trio of towels to a collection of motifs for heartwarming gift bags. On the other hand, if you prefer crafting, you'll find a host of fast-to-finish seasonal pleasers to create from a variety of materials. Choose your favorites and get set for compliments because you're certain to find just the right handmade tokens to give to all your special friends and neighbors!

Above and left—*This quartet of quick-to-complete gift bags will allow you to fashion favors that feature the "wrap." They'll be remembered long after paper wrapping and bows have been taken to the trash! Charts for Holiday Gift Bags are on page 98.*

Super Stitchery

This collection of cross-stitch designs, from delicate flowers to whimsical snowmen and adorable gingerbread men, is certain to warm your heart and have you humming favorite carols as you prepare for the season!

Everyone enjoys receiving presents packed in re-usable containers; and the *Holiday Gift Bags*, opposite, are real attention-getters! Worked in traditional seasonal colors, these gift holders can be used Christmas after Christmas. Stitch several in the weeks leading up to December 25th and you'll be able to assemble an attractive, appreciated gift at a moment's notice. Let the packaging be an important part of the presentation when you fill these bags with cellophane-wrapped cookies, candies, or other goodies. They'll be perfect for unexpected guests!

On this page, repeating borders and geometrics stitched with muted shades of floss create a delicate tapestry look on tiny *Victorian Christmas Stockings*. Tuck little surprises inside these darling miniatures and hang them on the tree. The treasures within will be enjoyed by all who receive them, and the stockings will be a reminder for seasons to come that you cared enough to share your time through your needlework.

For holiday stitchery with a whimsical flair, work the *Three Snowmen On A Towel* design. "Frosty" and friends romp across the band of a brightly colored cross-stitch fingertip towel you can

display in the powder room or kitchen. After all, you deserve a treat every now and then! Ideal, too, for last-minute giving, this appealing design, pictured on the next page, includes a trio of happy characters which will send out merry wishes season after season.

Also on the next page, the rose, a symbol of classic beauty, has been re-created as a motif that lends a distinctly feminine air to a pair of cross-stitch fingertip towels. Achieved in just a few hours, this stitchery is worked on linens that will be instant

Above—*Delicate floss colors form the stitched motifs for this set of miniature stockings. Great for use as "gift socks," these delightful pieces can be filled with small treasures and hung on the tree or displayed across a section of the mantel. Charts for* Victorian Christmas Stockings *begin on page 99.*

favorites with the ladies on your Christmas gift list.

If you know a special someone of school age, send her to class in style with a backpack and umbrella you can personalize as her very own! The backpack will hold everything she needs for her daily lessons, and the umbrella will help keep her dry on rainy school days. Adorn both with colorful balloons worked in primary brights, and watch her face light up when she opens your gift for her on Christmas morn!

Above—*A threesome of friendly snowmen adorns the band of a bright red, cross-stitch fingertip towel. Wonderful for giving or for keeping, these characters will impart a playful mood wherever they're displayed. Chart for* Three Snowmen On A Towel *is on page 102.*

Above right—*Beautiful roses decorate the bands of this set of cross-stitch fingertip towels. Work just one, or finish both to present to a friend who loves these breathtaking blooms. Chart for* Rose Motif Towels *is on page 101.*

Left—*Stitch sensational gifts for that dear little miss on your Christmas list. This simple cross stitch will transform practical accessories into charming pieces she can use for getting to and from school. Chart for* Balloons *backpack and umbrella is on page 101.*

94

Creative Crafting

If crafting is your favorite way to spend your free time, get set for plenty of fun as you create wonderful pieces to display in your own home or to present to all the special people on your gift-giving list!

Perhaps you love to decorate for the season with out-of-the-ordinary items. If so, the eye-catching *Grape Cluster Ornaments And Basket* will be positively perfect! An easy-to-make, "heat-needed" craft which yields fantastic results, the grape clusters are made from oven-hardening modeling compound, which is glued to purchased glass ball ornaments and a wicker basket. The grape motif strays from traditional red and green, making

this project marvelous for year-round display. Use the ornaments on evergreens during the yuletide season. When the time comes to dismantle the tree, remove the hangers and arrange the ornaments in the basket to create a centerpiece that's sure to please you and your guests. Craft these lovely pieces for use in your own home or give them to a friend who shares your preference for a touch of the unexpected during the Christmas season!

Whether you use handmade notepaper to enclose heartfelt greetings in your Christmas cards or to give with matching

envelopes as gifts, the lucky recipients are certain to be delighted. A super project for the first-time stenciler, *Stenciled Notepaper* pictured on page 96 will lend a unique beginning to seasonal messages of cheer.

Right and far right—Grape motifs transform purchased glass ball ornaments into trimmers which will adorn the tree in style and which will be equally as impressive when grouped together in a matching basket as an outstanding centerpiece. Instructions for Grape Cluster Ornaments And Basket *are on page 103.*

Above—The pretty poinsettia, a favorite at Christmastime, transforms plain paper into decorative notepaper. Instructions for Stenciled Notepaper *are on page 102.*

Do you fondly recall "galloping" up and down the sidewalks of your neighborhood with your stick horse when you were little? These *Hobby Horse Ornaments* will bring to mind those treasured days from your past. Use them to trim the tree or present them to your children and watch their eyes sparkle!

Fashioned after the church dolls from days gone by, *Handkerchief Dolls* are easy to craft and will provide quiet entertainment for youngsters who are just a little too young to sit quietly through the entire Christmas Eve service at church. Invite your little ones to join you in this simple crafting.

Consider yourself fortunate if you have inherited family treasures, such as old quilts, even if they're well-worn from use! With a little creativity, you can give a ragged quilt a second life when

Above—If you have youngsters eager to help with Christmas crafting, you can be sure these simple-to-make Hobby Horse Ornaments *will be a holiday hit. Made with felt, sequins, and a few basic craft items, this collection of ornaments will be a colorful, fun addition to the tree. Instructions begin on page 104.*

Above—Reminiscent of simpler days, these Handkerchief Dolls *were often used by mothers and grandmothers of the past to keep young children occupied and quiet during church services. Ideal for youngsters who are just a bit too young to sit for long without squirming or fidgeting, these dollies will make clever gift ideas for dedicated babysitters and Sunday school teachers! Instructions are on page 104.*

you salvage sections of it to use for making a noteworthy tree topper. Constructed from remnants of an old patchwork quilt, which had done its duty for generations keeping family members cozy, this star features buttonhole stitching, which binds the front and back pieces together. This project offers a splendid way to use sections of this tattered keepsake to preserve cherished family memories. The star will allow you to continue the tradition of passing down heirlooms, which represent family history to future generations.

We all like quick and inexpensive gifts we can fashion from things we have on hand. Scraps of lace fabric can be easily transformed into lovely *Sachets Of Lace*, perfect for filling with small scented soaps or potpourri.

Decorate every inch of your home for the holidays with these over-sized *Doorknob Jingle Bells*. They'll add a festive touch to every area of your home when hung on doorknobs throughout the house and they'll make great gifts, too!

Above—Made from scraps of lace and filled with soaps, potpourri, or other sweet things, these Sachets Of Lace *will make elegant gifts at Christmas as well as birthdays and bridal showers. Instructions are on page 103.*

Above left and right—Doorknob Jingle Bells *in festive colors can be used to add a touch of the holidays in every room. Delightful as decorating pieces, these doorknob adornments can also be pleasing presents! Instructions are on page 104.*

Left—Made from the remnants of an old tattered quilt, this unique tree topper is certain to make your guests take a second look. If you have inherited an old quilt that is no longer usable, salvage the less-worn spots and use them to create unforgettable heirlooms for each of your siblings. Instructions for Cutter Quilt Star *are on page 103.*

Holiday Gift Bags

DMC	Color
X	321	red
Z	699	green
● white	white
╱	436	tan
bs	938	coffee, ul.dk.

Fabric: 14-count antique white Aida from Zweigart®

Stitch count:

Candy Canes   12H x 39W
Gingerbread Men   16H x 35W
Do Not Open   12H x 39W
With Love At Christmas 14H x 32W

Design size:

Candy Canes
14-count   ⅞" x 2¾"
Gingerbread Men
14-count   1⅛" x 2½"
Do Not Open
14-count   ⅞" x 2¾"
With Love At Christmas
14-count   1" x 2¼"

Note: Cut fabric for *Candy Canes* and *Do Not Open* 6½" x 6". Cut fabric for *Gingerbread Men* and *With Love At Christmas* 6½" x 5½". For each design, measure up 2" from bottom of fabric and mark. This line marks placement for bottom of cross-stitch design. Fold fabric in half lengthwise to find center.

Instructions: Cross stitch using two strands of floss. Backstitch using one strand of floss unless otherwise indicated. Make French knots using two strands of floss, wrapping floss around needle twice.

Backstitch (bs) instructions:

699   candy canes, *Do Not Open, With love at Christmas*
321   *until Dec. 25th* (two strands)
white   bands on gingerbread men's arms and legs
938   gingerbread men

French knot instructions:

938   gingerbread men's buttons
699   gingerbread men's eyes

Materials:

Scraps of fabric in holiday colors **or** Aida scraps (for backing)
Thread to match
Assorted ribbons and lace trim
Disappearing ink fabric marking pen
Sewing machine (optional)
Straight pins
Scissors
Iron

1. Complete all cross stitch following instructions given.

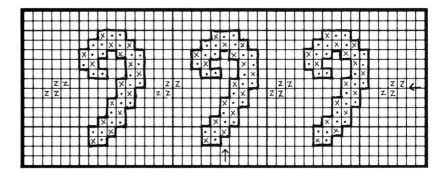

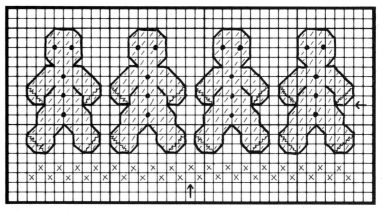

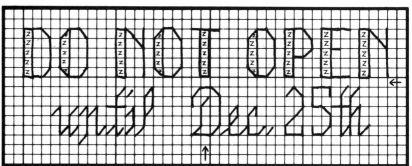

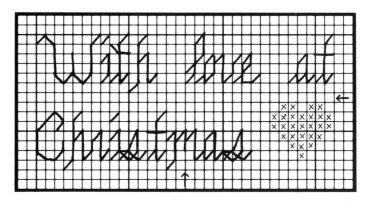

2. Finished size for each gift bag will be determined by stitch count of each design and by fabric used. To mark seam lines, count equal numbers of squares out from the edges of each cross-stitch design on the bottom and both sides, leaving a ½" seam allowance. Mark with disappearing ink fabric marking pen on wrong side of fabric, following "track" of fabric to achieve straight lines.

3. Cut fabric backing pieces to fit bag front pieces.

4. With right sides together, center fabric backing pieces over completed cross-stitch designs. Pin.

5. Stitch along markings for seam lines. Trim seams and clip corners. Turn and press.

6. Turn top raw edges under and press. Machine stitch or hand stitch lace trim around top edges of bags.

7. Fill bags with small presents or treats and tie tops closed with ribbon.

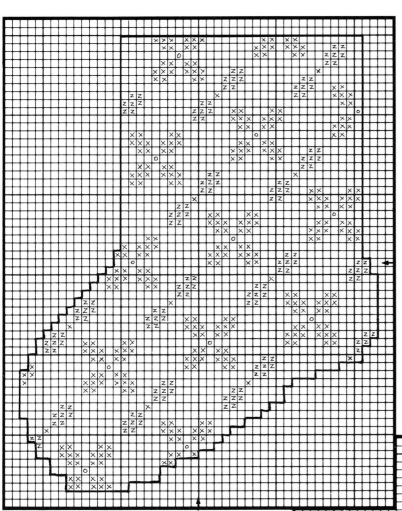

STOCKING 1

Fabric: 27-count cream linen from Norden Crafts
Stitch count: 57H x 46W
Design size:
14-count   4⅛" x 3¼"
18-count   3⅛" x 2½"
25-count   4½" x 3⅝"
27-count   4¼" x 3⅜"

Instructions: Cross stitch over two threads using two strands of floss. Backstitch using one strand of floss unless otherwise indicated.

Backstitch (bs) instructions:

640	*Stocking 1*
502	lines inside *Stocking 2* (two strands)
640	remainder of backstitching on *Stocking 2*
932	*Stocking 3*
502	lettering and year on *Stocking 4* (two strands)
640	remainder of backstitching on *Stocking 4*

Victorian Christmas Stockings

DMC	Color
	Stocking 1	
X	223	pink, med.
o	676	old gold, lt.
Z	502	blue-green
bs	640	beige-gray, vy. dk.
	Stocking 2	
X	932	antique blue, lt.
Z	760	salmon
bs	502	blue-green
bs	640	beige-gray, vy. dk.
	Stocking 3	
X	932	antique blue, lt.
	Stocking 4	
Z	932	antique blue, lt.
o	676	old gold, lt.
╱	3042	antique violet, lt.
X	502	blue-green
3	223	pink, med.
·	775	baby blue, lt.
bs	640	beige-gray, vy. dk.

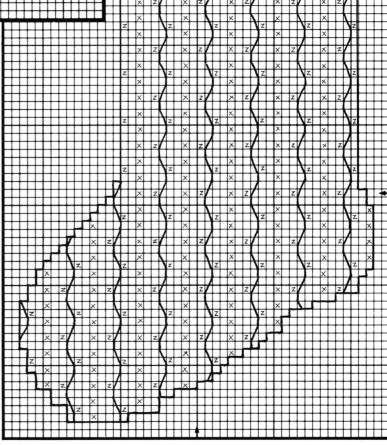

STOCKING 2

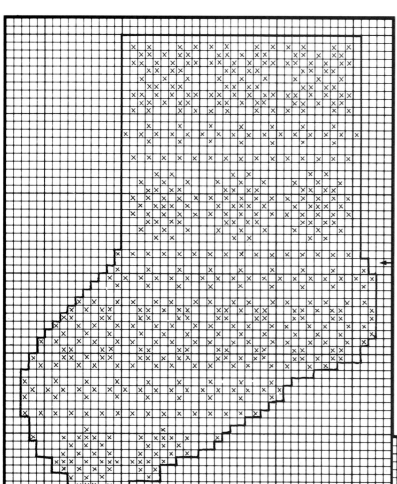

STOCKING 3

and following outline of stocking shape when tacking. Continue around perimeter of outline, including top of stocking. Repeat for remaining stitched fronts.

4. Place each stitched front with a backing piece, placing right sides together, and pin. Stitch pieces together, using previous stitching line as a guide but leaving top of stocking open. Trim seams and turn stockings right-side out. At top of each stocking, fold raw edges under twice and stitch to make a narrow hem. Fold hem to inside of stocking and press, using outline across top of stocking as a guide for folding.

5. To finish, fold 6"-length of ribbon in half to form hanging loop and tack ribbon ends to inside back of stocking at upper right-hand corner. Repeat for remaining stockings.

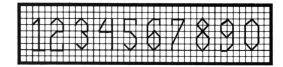

Materials:
¼ yd. 44/45"-wide muslin **or** complementary fabric of your choice (for backing)
Thread to match
⅝ yd. ⅛"-wide ivory satin ribbon, cut into 6" lengths (for hangers)
Measuring tape
Hand-sewing needle
Scissors
Straight pins
Sewing machine (optional)

1. Complete all cross stitch following instructions given.
2. Cut eight 4½" x 6" pieces of muslin. Four pieces will be used to line stitched front, and four pieces will be used for backing.
Note: We chose to line the stitched fronts since the cross-stitch designs were worked on a loose-weave linen.
3. To line, place one piece of muslin to back side of each stitched front. Tack muslin and stitched front together, forming one piece of fabric with which to work

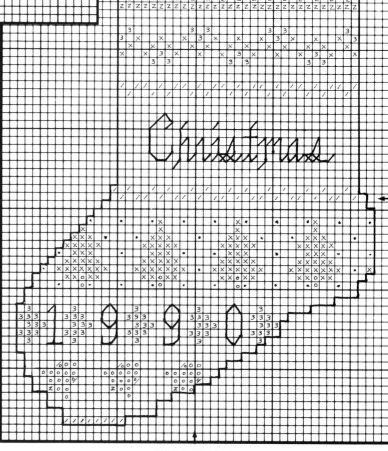

STOCKING 4

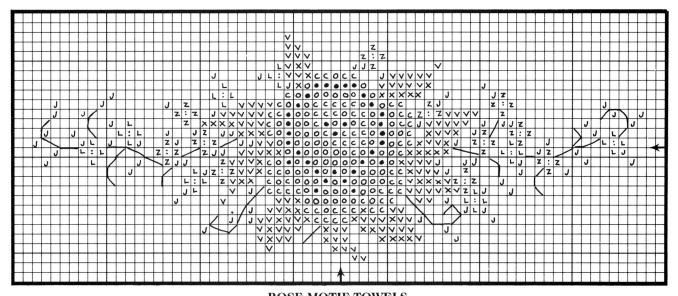

ROSE MOTIF TOWELS

Rose Motif Towels

DMC	Color
● 3687	mauve
○ 3688	mauve, med.
C 3689	mauve, lt.
: 744	yellow, pl.
L 794	cornflower, lt.
Z 793	cornflower, med.
V 368	pistachio, lt.
X 367	pistachio, dk.
J 3053	green-gray

Fabric: 14-count blue mist twill and 14-count pink soufflé twill Borderlines Fingertips towels from Charles Craft, Inc.
Stitch count: 24H x 66W
Design size:

11-count	2⅛" x 6"
14-count	1¾" x 4¾"
18-count	1⅜" x 3⅝"
22-count	1⅛" x 3"

Instructions: Cross stitch using three strands of floss. Backstitch using two strands 3053.

Balloons

DMC	Color
Backpack	
L 796	royal blue, dk.
Z white	white
V 911	emerald, med.
= 744	yellow, pl.

Umbrella	
L white	white
Z 321	red
V 911	emerald, med.
= 744	yellow, pl.

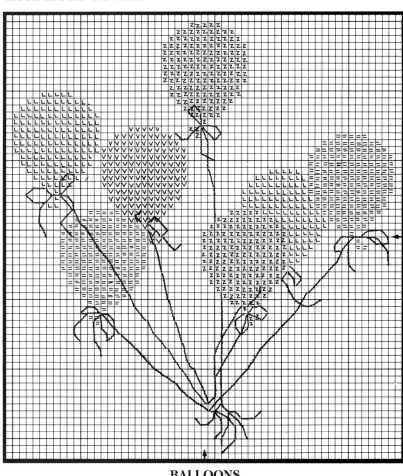

BALLOONS

Fabric: 10-count waste canvas from Zweigart®

Stitch count: 62H x 57W
Design size:

10-count	6¼" x 5⅝"
14-count	4½" x 4⅛"

Instructions: Cross stitch using five strands of floss. Backstitch using two strands 801.

Note: Should you wish to stitch this design on another color, change the balloon colors to suit the background.

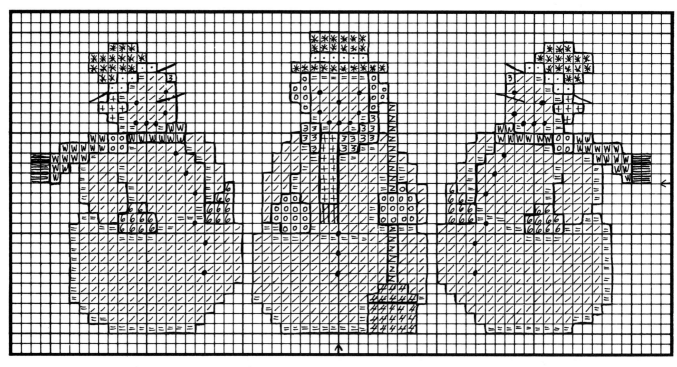

THREE SNOWMEN ON A TOWEL

Three Snowmen On A Towel

	DMC	Color
∕	white	white
=	762	pearl gray, vy. lt.
✳	310	black
3	304	red, med.
+	321	red
W	699	green
o	701	green, lt.
•	973	canary, bt.
Z	433	brown, med.
6	798	delft, dk.
4	783	gold
ss	971	pumpkin

Fabric: 14-count red Park Avenue Fingertips Towel from Charles Craft, Inc.
Stitch count: 30H x 64W
Design size:

11-count	2¾" x 5¾"
14-count	2⅛" x 4⅝"
18-count	1⅝" x 3½"
22-count	1⅜" x 2⅞"

Instructions: Cross stitch using two strands of floss. Backstitch using two strands of floss unless otherwise indicated. Straight stitch using one strand of floss unless otherwise indicated. Make French knots for snowmen's eyes and buttons using two strands 310, wrapping floss around needle twice.
Backstitch instructions:

310 hat brims, broom, snowmen (one strand)
433 band on broom

Straight stitch (ss) instructions:

971 carrot noses (two strands)
699 green scarf tassels
321 red scarf tassels

Stenciled Notepaper

Materials:
One 6" x 6" sheet Mylar®
Craft knife
Fine point permanent marker
Small stencil brush
Tracing paper
Stencil paint: red, green
Yellow acrylic paint
Palette
Size 0 paintbrush
Masking tape
Cutting board   Paper towels
Notepaper and envelopes

1. Trace patterns onto tracing paper.
2. Cut Mylar® in half. Tape pattern to cutting board and place Mylar® over pattern, rough-side down. Tape Mylar® in place and, using craft knife, cut out pattern. (Smooth side will be right side of stencil.) Transfer dots in stencil #2 to Mylar® with permanent marker.
3. Place stencil #1 on notepaper, referring to photo for placement. Tape in place.
4. Place small amount of green paint on palette. Dip stencil brush into paint and work into brush thoroughly. Blot excess on paper towels. The brush

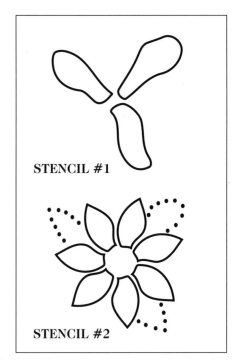

STENCIL #1

STENCIL #2

should have very little paint in it. Apply paint with circular motion until you have desired color. Remove stencil and let dry.

5. Place stencil #2 in position and tape in place. (Dots on stencil #2 indicate edges of leaves on stencil #1.) Apply red paint in same manner as for green paint. Remove stencil and let dry.

6. Put several yellow and red dots in center of flower, using size 0 paintbrush.

Grape Cluster Ornaments And Basket

Materials:
Glass Christmas balls in color of your choice
Wicker basket
Oven-hardening modeling compound
Acrylic paint: dark blue, light blue
Water base satin varnish
Green paper twist cord
Tacky glue
Sharp knife
Paintbrushes: one small, one fine
Aluminum pan
Oven

1. Shape modeling compound into small rolls. Cut thin circles and place on aluminum pan. Bake at 250°F until dry.
2. Glue circles onto Christmas balls and basket, forming grape clusters.
3. Unwind green paper twist cord and cut leaves and stem for each grape cluster. Glue on.
4. Paint grapes dark blue, using small brush. When dry, highlight with light blue. Paint veins in leaves, using fine brush and light blue paint.
5. Apply two coats of varnish to grapes, leaves, and stems.

Sachets Of Lace

Materials:
Assorted lace scraps with selvage edges
Thread to match
Ribbon scraps
Tailor's chalk
Sewing machine
Measuring tape
Straight pins
Scissors
Iron

Note: The finished sizes of the sachets shown on page 97 are 3" x 5½" (small), 3½" x 6¼" (medium), and 5½" x 8" (large).

1. Determine desired size for finished sachet. Double the width and add a ⅜" seam allowance at bottom and sides to determine size to cut lace scrap.
2. Mark lace scrap lightly with tailor's chalk, following straight grain, and cut out. Fold in half with right sides together and with selvage edges together at top. Pin.
3. Stitch across the bottom and up the open side, backstitching for added reinforcement at corner and using a ⅜" seam allowance. Trim seams. Turn and press. If using sheer lace, such as that used for

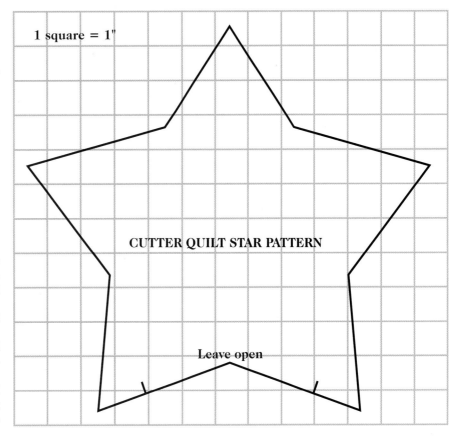

1 square = 1"

CUTTER QUILT STAR PATTERN

Leave open

models shown, trim excess sheer fabric from top, using scallops as cutting guide.
4. Fill with decorative soaps or potpourri and tie top closed with ribbon.

Cutter Quilt Star

Materials:
Two 12" squares of damaged patchwork quilt
3 yds. Persian wool
Crewel needle with large eye
Polyester filling
Straight pins
Scissors

Note: If new patchwork is used, add seam allowance to pattern and sew star with right sides together. Trim seam allowance and turn. Hand hem open edges.

1. Enlarge star pattern as indicated. Cut out.
2. Pin pattern to right side of patchwork square. Cut around pattern. Mark opening on right side of fabric, as indicated on pattern. Remove pattern. Repeat for second patchwork square.
3. Place wrong sides of stars together. Work buttonhole stitch to bind edges, using two strands of wool and leaving opening in bottom as marked so star will

slip over treetop. Pull strands of wool through patchwork fabric gently, as old quilts tear easily.
4. Stuff small amounts of polyester filling into star points.
5. Finish opening in bottom of star with buttonhole stitch.

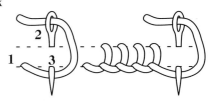

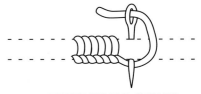

BUTTONHOLE STITCH

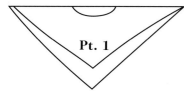

DIAGRAM 1

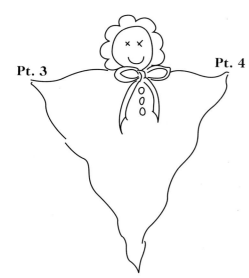

DIAGRAM 2

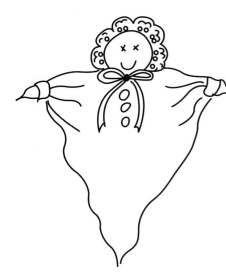

DIAGRAM 3

Handkerchief Dolls

Materials:

1 white handkerchief, approximately 10" x 12" (for **each** doll—depending on the size doll you wish to make, larger or smaller handkerchiefs may be used.)

3 small buttons in color of your choice (for **each** doll)

6"-length ¾"-wide, pre-gathered white lace (for **each** doll)

12"-length ⅛"-wide satin ribbon in color of your choice (for **each** doll)

1 skein embroidery floss, color: DMC 776

1 skein embroidery floss, color: DMC 3325

Hand-sewing needle (for working eyes and mouth)

Thread (optional, for tacking bow)

Measuring tape

Powder blush

Cotton swab

Fabric marker

Scissors

Note: When making dolls for very young children, omit buttons.

1. Fold handkerchief into a triangle, placing point 1 approximately 3½" from point 2 (Diagram 1).

2. Place two cotton balls under the semicircle area (Diagram 1) and gather in hand. Using fabric marker, mark location for each eye and mouth. Unfold handkerchief and remove cotton balls.

3. Work a freehand cross stitch over marking for each eye, using four strands DMC 3325. Work freehand outline stitch over marking for mouth, using four strands DMC 776.

4. Place cotton balls under semicircle, re-gather, and secure tightly with satin ribbon, tying ribbon into a bow under chin. (Secure bow by tacking at center with needle and thread, if desired. This will prevent bow from coming untied when doll is handled.)

5. Whipstitch lace around face to achieve a bonnet effect.

6. Stitch buttons below ribbon (Diagram 2).

7. Tie a loose knot at point 3 and at point 4 to form hands (Diagrams 2 and 3).

8. To complete, use cotton swab to apply a very light amount of powder blush to doll's cheeks.

Doorknob Jingle Bells

Materials:

Two large 3½"-diameter jingle bells

3⅓ yds. 3.5mm macramé cord (for **each** bell)

Floral wire

1 yd. ½"-wide ribbon (for **each** bell)

Christmas greenery and decorations (for trim)

Measuring tape

Glue gun

Tape

Note: Materials listed will make two *Doorknob Jingle Bells.*

1. For **each** bell, cut cord into six 20"-long pieces. On both ends, tape two 20" pieces, or strands, of cord together and repeat for remaining strands. (Each of these two combined strands of cord will form one cord in braid.)

2. Wire three taped cords (six strands) together at one end and tape to a flat surface. Braid. When finished, trim braided cord for each bell to 12" long. Thread braided cord through hanger on top of each bell. Wire ends together.

3. Slip joined, braided cord ends around to each bell hanger and glue to conceal wired ends.

4. Glue Christmas greenery and decorations at top of each bell as desired.

5. Make bows, referring to "How-Tos For Making A Bow" on page 105, and glue at top of each bell, as desired.

Hobby Horse Ornaments

Materials:

Four 9" x 12" pieces red felt

1 pkg. small gold sequins

2 yds. gold cord, cut into 5" lengths (for hangers)

Fourteen 6"-long candy canes (**each** with one curled end)

Tacky glue

Sewing machine

Measuring tape

Red thread

Hand-sewing needle

Scissors

Pencil

Note: Materials listed will make fourteen *Hobby Horse Ornaments.*

1. Pin pattern to felt and trace around pattern edges. Repeat to make twenty-eight pieces. Cut out.
2. Pin two felt pieces together, aligning edges. Stitch together, using a ⅛" seam and leaving bottom open.
3. Glue sequins on dots.
4. Thread needle with 5" length of gold cord, sew through felt at top of bridle, and tie a knot in cord ends to form hanger.
5. Insert curled end of candy cane.
6. Repeat #2-#5 for remaining ornaments.

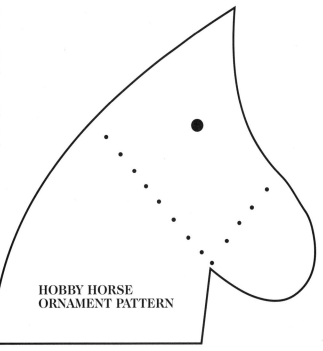

HOBBY HORSE
ORNAMENT PATTERN

How-Tos For Making A Bow

Materials:
Ribbon, as listed in materials list for project being made
Wire, as listed in materials list for project being made
Ruler   Scissors

Note: These instructions include the general technique used for making a bow. The dimensions included in these instructions are calculated for 1½ yds. of ribbon and a 6"-length of wire for each bow. For another yardage, you will need to re-calculate the measurements used. For a fuller look, you will need to re-calculate both the yardage needed and the measurements used. Lay ruler flat on work surface for measuring. Use both hands to hold ribbon.

1. To make first "streamer," measure 3" of ribbon (do not cut) and crimp edges together at this point. This crimped area will be center of bow.
2. To make first loop, hold crimped area between thumb and forefinger, with right side facing you. Measure 4" of remaining ribbon, bring to back of center, crimp edges together, and twist ribbon so right side is up. This loop will be to the left of the bow's center.

Note: Each time you bring a loop to the center, you must twist the ribbon so that the right side will be up for the next loop.

3. To make second loop, continue to hold center as indicated. Measure 4" of remaining ribbon, bring to back of center, crimp edges together, and twist ribbon over so right side of ribbon is up. This loop will be to the right of the bow's center.

4. Continue making loops on left and right of bow's center until there are five loops on either side. Always bring crimped ribbon to back of bow.

Note: Some of the projects featured in this book include bows which have more than five loops on either side of the center. Make adjustments as needed to achieve desired effect.

5. Let second "streamer" stick out with right side facing you.
6. Secure center of bow (crimped area) with wire, twisting tightly.
7. Beginning on one side of center, pull one loop up and one loop down until each loop is in a pleasing position. Repeat for other side.
8. Trim ends of "streamers" and attach bow to project as indicated using wire.
9. Repeat for remaining bows.

STEP 1

STEP 2

STEP 3

STEP 4

STEP 5

1632

la petite

85¢

Washable
P20-1/2" 6 On

CRAFT WITH SCRAPS

If you enjoy crafts that are inexpensive and quick-to-complete, yet have such style that you would be proud to use them in your own home or as gifts, this collection of fashions for decorating and wearing will fill your needs! From appliqué suitable for all ages to plaid handcrafts that will tickle your fancy, you're certain to find a variety of things on the following pages that you'll want to make. The best thing about most of these projects is that they can be assembled by combining a few purchased pieces with scraps of fabric and other craft items—those tidbits of calico, those snippets of felt, those odds and ends you just couldn't bring yourself to throw away. Dig all the way to the bottom of your sewing basket and get busy preparing for the season ahead!

CRAFT WITH SCRAPS

Quick Quilting

There's just something about the country that suggests warmth and friendliness, and nothing spells down-home goodness more than calico prints and muslin. These *Miniature Quilt Ornaments* are certain to convey a pleasing hint of rural charm in your decorating. Worked entirely by hand, these darling branch trimmers will be ideal projects for both experienced quilters and enthusiastic beginners. Why not quilt these with your child or your grandchild? It's a great way to capture quality time together, to include the younger set in seasonal preparations, and to start children on a first quilting project. These quilts are just the right size to be finished in time for Christmas gift-giving.

From teddy bears to holly leaves, these tree adornments are sure to delight! Instructions for Miniature Quilt Ornaments are on page 125.

CRAFT WITH SCRAPS

Felt & Fabric Fashions

From quick, easy appliqué to fun with fusible web, you'll find a host of favorites on the following pages to make and give for Christmas!

Any young boy will absolutely adore these sweaters, each of which sports a wonderful appliqué design for the holidays. In fact, these sweaters embellished with the *Drum And Soldier Appliqué* are suitable to wear throughout the winter! By combining felt scraps with purchased sweaters and using simple machine appliqué, you can create these royal charmers for your children. These appliqué designs also

***Above and right**—Machine appliqué can be used to create an assortment of seasonal pieces, from* Sweaters For The Boys, *above, to* Easy Appliqué Pillows, *right. Instructions for* Drum And Soldier Appliqué *begin on page 125.*

provide a great way to transform a plain, hand-me-down sweater outgrown by an older brother into a second-hand treat that will rank first-rate with the youngest who receives it!

Use these versatile motifs on other items as well. The shirred cording pillows will bring Christmas cheer to any room, and the designs can also be made into ornaments to add a regal touch to the evergreen.

This gathering of reindeer may not possess Rudolph's fame, but it's sure to be a hit this holiday season! When the designer of these precious lovables first put pen to paper to make *Happy Holidays Reindeer*, more than a half-dozen uses for this single pattern came to mind. She then started to work and created everything from wearing apparel and unique accessories to a paper garland and gift bags. Use her suggestions or challenge your imagination for countless hours of crafting fun!

Above—A trio of reindeer frolic across the front of this Prancing Reindeer Sweatshirt. *Instructions begin on page 126.*

Above—The whimsical reindeer takes on an unexpected formality on a rich Ultrasuede® belt used to accessorize dressy, holiday apparel. *Instructions for* Ultrasuede® Reindeer Belt *are on page 128.*

Above—A single reindeer, stuffed and finished as a pin, will dance across a lapel or blouse pocket in unforgettable style. *Instructions for* Reindeer Pin *are on page 128.*

Below and left—For holiday accessories with casual appeal, the versatile reindeer design perfectly complements the Lined Reindeer Belt. These arctic friends, finished as a Reindeer Scarf Slide, will add just the right finishing touch to a basic scarf, transforming it into a unique accessory. Attach to the scarf slide and the same friendly fellows form a festive Reindeer Necklace, left. Wear your favorite combination the next time you head for the mall and be prepared for second glances! Instructions for Lined Reindeer Belt, Reindeer Scarf Slide, and Reindeer Necklace begin on page 126.

Above—Happy Reindeer Gift Bags package tiny treasures in a merry manner, and they can be used over and over again. For tree decorations with a playful flair, use kraft paper and a few other crafting basics to create the Prancing Reindeer Paper Garland. Instructions are on page 126.

113

Accessories make the outfit, and these reindeer accessories, from an attention-getting necklace to a conversation-starting lapel pin, are sure to make your holiday look. To add a new twist to a trusted standby, try a festive Ultrasuede® belt with a plaid skirt and lacy blouse. The same belt pattern takes on a decidedly different look when made with woven fabric and lined. Pair the fabric belt with a complementary scarf and matching scarf slide for the perfect accent for a casual holiday gathering.

And don't stop with wearables. The reindeer pattern is great for wraps and trims as well. Put these darling deer on basic brown paper bags or fancier bags with colorful prints for the simplest, fastest gift wrap. Although these bags won't hide their contents completely from prying hands, they'll work fine to hold surprises for less curious folks on your Christmas list. And for trimming the tree, just a

Top and above—A white sweatshirt and a pair of tees take on Christmassy appeal when appliquéd with popular seasonal motifs. Instructions for Quick And Easy Appliqué Shirts, *begin on page 128.*

114

little creative work with your scissors will yield the appealing *Prancing Reindeer Paper Garland*.

Do you admire the T-shirts and sweatshirts you see others wearing each year at Christmastime but cringe at department store prices? Well, this *Quick And Easy Appliqué* is ideal for you! Just a few, simple designs are all you'll need to create an entire collection of fabulous wearables.

The red T-shirt sports a plaid taffeta Christmas tree, complete with packages, a golden star, and tiny jingle bell ornaments. The star, garland, and bows on the packages are "drawn" on with glitter paint. The gold T is decorated with oversized gift boxes. Trimmed with gold and silver metallic rickrack and edged with glitter paint, the packages will keep you dreaming about the surprises in store for you! The white sweatshirt boasts an array of holly leaves in assorted sizes and fabrics. Here they enhance the yoke of this cozy sweatshirt, but you can achieve a completely different look when you arrange them randomly to create patterns of your choice. Tack on small red buttons for holly berries and you're set for the season!

The holly leaf patterns can also be used to make a variety of decorative items for the home, such as the *Wreath Of Holly Pillow* and the place mat and napkin sets pictured on this page.

Above—*The holly leaf design can be used to turn plain, purchased table linens into dinnertime delights. Instructions for* Quick And Easy Appliqué Table Linens, *begin on page 128. Instructions for* Fabric Napkin Rings, *which complete the place setting, are on page 130.*

Above—*Create a colorful home-decorating item using a Christmas classic—the holly leaf. Place the fabric leaves as shown to create the* Wreath Of Holly Pillow *or experiment as you wish to create your own interesting pieces. Instructions begin on page 128.*

Above—*A mother sheep and her little lamb make a heartwarming pair, created with faux pearls and Ultrasuede® on the front of a purchased pullover sweater. Completed with a polka-dot ribbon and meandering streamers of pearls at one shoulder, this Christmas charmer will be the best present under the tree! Instructions for Pearly Sheep begin on page 130.*

Festive Wearables

Here's a sweater suited for dual duty! Perfect for taking you from day wear into the evening in smashing style, it can be worn throughout this merriest of all seasons. Create the *Pearly Sheep* sweater,

pictured opposite, using a purchased sweater, faux pearls, tiny scraps of Ultrasuede®, and complementary ribbon. Wear it to top off slacks for a winning daytime look, or pair it with a black velvet skirt

for a nighttime knockout!

On this page, a knitted yoke with rolled collar makes an extra-cozy creation when it's worked onto a sweatshirt like this one. Made with cotton yarn (and apologies to

our wool-bearing friends), this yoke features "woolly" white sheep lined up between borders of pink hearts and yellow diamonds! Why not make this *Sheep In A Row Sweatshirt* for a special someone on your gift list? It's sure to be her favorite present.

Whether you're dashing through the mall to finish your last-minute shopping or attending a get-together with friends, you're going to turn heads when you don this adorable *HO HO HO Sweater.* You say you don't know how to knit? Well, surprise! This look was achieved in duplicate stitch on a purchased stockinette-stitch sweater. You can re-create it on a sweater of your choice, even one from your closet.

The design can also be cross-stitched and framed for a fun-to-display decorating item. Those devoted solely to cross stitch will be glad to know we've incorporated those instructions, too!

Also on this page is a holiday-green sweatshirt that will be splendid for welcoming the yuletide season. Trimmed with yo-yo quilt circles, this top features the products of this quilting technique in classic Christmas colors. When the circles are made from fabrics of non-traditional hues and used to embellish a matching sweatshirt, you can wear your creation throughout the cooler months of the year, as well, to proclaim your love for this endearing needle craft.

Above—*Yo-yo quilting transforms a plain sweatshirt into casual attire with a special flair for the holidays. For additional yo-yo quilting ideas, turn to page 42. Instructions for Yo-yo Creations—Sweatshirt, are on page 43.*

Left—*Worked in duplicate stitch on a purchased navy sweater, this stitchery is certain to prompt a smile from all who glimpse it. Instructions for HO HO HO Sweater begin on page 132.*

Page 117—*If you knit, why not make this charming yoke for a sweatshirt to present to a favorite niece on your Christmas gift list? Instructions for Sheep In A Row Sweatshirt are on page 134.*

Mad For Plaid

Do you love the charm of traditional and not-so-traditional plaids? Well, if you possess a passion for this pleasing pattern or simply a fondness for it, you'll find seasonal delights in this collection of plaid holiday-inspired designs!

Plaid is available in a wide selection of fabrics, from soft cotton to heavy wool to oh-so-elegant taffeta, but there's something especially cozy about plaid flannel. If you remember the cold winters from your childhood, and how your mother would bundle you up in layer upon layer of clothing, you will also recall that there was nothing better than the soft, slightly fuzzy texture of a plaid flannel shirt keeping you cuddled in warmth against the biting air. Allow that traditional plaid to be a comfort to you today by finding new uses for it in pillowcases, in star-shaped ornaments, and in a variety of other items. Limited only by your imagination, plaid can hold a one-of-a-kind, holiday flair.

Make a posh entrance at the next Christmas party when you arrive dressed in plaid taffeta. These designs provide an inexpensive way to make your very own seasonal fashions, and you can be pretty certain your outfit will be different from everyone else's! Pictured on page 120 is a one-size-fits-all, pleated skirt. The pattern

Above—Perfect covers for pillows you'll use while relaxing with a book, napping, or watching television, these Cozy Flannel Pillowcases *will make your pillow especially inviting! Instructions begin on page 135.*

119

Above and above left—*Dress for the party in eye-catching style with winning plaid wearables. Instructions for Holiday Finery, above left, begin on page 137. Instructions for Star-Studded Sweater, above, are on page 139.*

is simple, and you can adapt it to fit whoever will wear the finished garment.

The five-pointed star was used to grace a dressy sweater, shown worn atop a red and black plaid split skirt, near left. The plaid split skirt was made using a commercial pattern (see page 139 for pattern information); and the stars were made with fabric left over from the split skirt, with a few scraps of silver lamé added. Appliqué the stars to a complementary purchased sweater to complete your ensemble, and you'll be ready for most any occasion.

Pictured on this page is a trio of wool tartan pillows that have been finished with ribbon to resemble wrapped packages. Ideal for giving, these toss pillows are quick to complete and can be used long after Christmas has passed by removing the ribbon bows and felt gift tags. For pillows with added charm, shop for bright red corduroy and classic black-and-white houndstooth check. Appliquéd with an assortment of scraps from your sewing basket to form charming designs, these pieces are certain to be adored.

Above right—These Wool Tartan Pillows With Gift Tags *will make wonderful accent pieces during the holidays, and when the tags are removed, these decorative pillows can be used throughout the winter months. Instructions are on page 136.*

Right—For ready-in-a-flash gifts, purchase hand towels in seasonal colors and trim them with colorful scraps of plaid fabric. Instructions for Super Quick Plaid Gifts *are on page 135.*

If you are the hostess of the festivities, you'll want to protect your finery from any last-minute kitchen mishaps—and what better way to do so than with a holiday-colored apron decorated with plaid stars? The star shape shows its versatility and allows a plain apron to become a festive fashion statement.

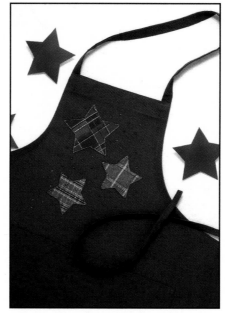

Above—Protect your Christmas fashions from spills while allowing your enthusiasm for the season to shine through with an apron decorated for the holidays. Instructions for Holiday Apron *are on page 136.*

Right—Popular motifs, machine-appliquéd to houndstooth-check fabric squares, form appealing button-on fronts for red corduroy throw pillows. Instructions for Button-on Pillows *begin on page 136.*

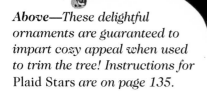

Above—These delightful ornaments are guaranteed to impart cozy appeal when used to trim the tree! Instructions for Plaid Stars *are on page 135.*

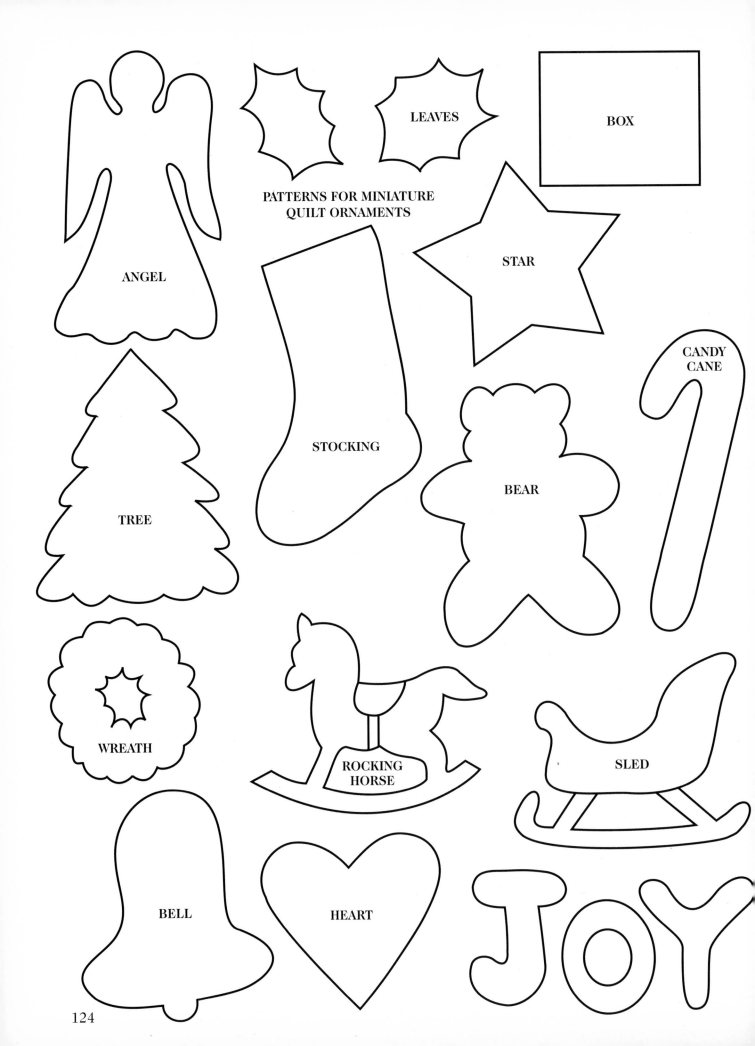

LEAVES

BOX

PATTERNS FOR MINIATURE
QUILT ORNAMENTS

ANGEL

STAR

CANDY
CANE

STOCKING

TREE

BEAR

WREATH

ROCKING
HORSE

SLED

BELL

HEART

JOY

124

Miniature Quilt Ornaments

Materials:

Assorted fabric scraps (calicoes, stripes, etc.)

Scraps of ¼"-wide ribbon in assorted colors

Scrap of lace

14 small red chenille balls

¼ yd. thin batting

¼ yd. 44/45"-wide muslin

Pellon® Wonder-Under™ Transfer Web

Graphite paper

4 yds. narrow cord, cut into 10"-12" lengths (for hangers)

Thread to match muslin

Measuring tape

Hand-sewing needle

Scissors

Iron

Note: Muslin may be soaked in tea for an aged appearance. However, this process weakens the fabric and will affect the life of the finished ornament.

1. Transfer pattern to Wonder-Under™, using graphite paper. Cut out. Cut a piece of calico 1" larger than pattern to be used. Fuse Wonder-Under™ to wrong side of calico, following manufacturer's instructions for fusing.
2. Cut a 2½" x 3½" piece of muslin. Peel paper from design and fuse design onto muslin.
3. Cut a 2½" x 3½" piece of batting.
4. Cut calico 3½" x 4½". Place atop flat surface wrong-side up. Center batting and muslin on top and pin.
5. Quilt around muslin ¼" from edge. Fold calico over muslin and blind stitch in place, keeping edges straight and even.
6. Quilt around design.
7. Refer to pages 108 and 109 for trim placement. Make ribbon bows and tack to wreath, candy cane, bell, package, and teddy bear. Tack three chenille balls between holly leaves for berries. Tack chenille balls to Christmas tree for ornaments. Tack lace and ribbon to stocking.
8. Tack on cord, as desired, for hangers, tying small bows at cord ends.

Drum And Soldier Appliqué

Sweaters For The Boys
Materials:

Two purchased sweaters of your choice

High-quality washable felt scraps: red, royal blue, flesh, white, black, gold

Thread to match sweaters and felt scraps

9"x 12" piece gray felt (for base of appliqué)

½ yd. Pellon® Wonder-Under™ Transfer Web

¼ yd. Pellon® Stretch-Ease™ **or** Sof-Shape™ interfacing

½ yd. ⅛"-wide green satin ribbon

6 black seed beads (for soldiers' eyes)

22 4-mm gold beads (7 for drum, 15 for soldiers)

7" metallic gold thread (for hangers)

Beading needle

Hand-sewing needle

Pencil

Scissors

Sewing machine   Press cloth

Measuring tape   Iron

Note: Patterns shown actual size. Yardage listed will make models as shown. Sweaters shown are boys' size 10-12. Appliquéd soldiers are 5" tall, and drum is 4¾" high at tallest point. Enlarge patterns if desired, making sure to re-calculate the materials needed before purchasing. Prewash washable felt and sweaters before appliquéing to check for colorfastness.

1. To make appliqué motifs, trace patterns onto paper side of Wonder-Under™. Fuse Wonder-Under™ to felt pieces, following manufacturer's instructions for fusing. Cut out shapes, peel off paper backing, and arrange felt pieces, referring to photo on page 110 for placement. Fuse design to gray felt base, leaving ⅛"

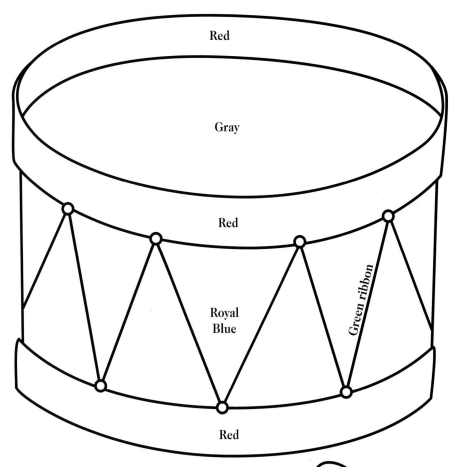

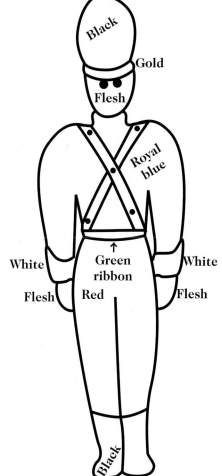

of gray around perimeter of design. Set sewing machine to straight stitch and, with matching thread, machine sew around all felt shapes 1/16" in from edge of each piece.

2. Sew green ribbon across soldiers' waists for belts, across soldiers' chests for suspenders, and in zigzag shape around drum (refer to pattern for placement). Sew gold beads at points of ribbon on drum and on suspenders of soldiers. Sew black beads on soldiers' faces for eyes.

3. Fuse Wonder-Under™ onto back side of appliqué motifs. Cut out shape, leaving approximately 3/16" of gray felt showing around perimeter of each design. Fuse appliqués to sweaters, using a press cloth. On inside of sweaters, fuse interfacing behind appliqué areas to reinforce. Machine-stitch appliqués onto sweaters, following edges of motifs and using gray thread.

Easy Appliqué Pillows
Materials:
Four 18" x 18" squares royal blue fabric
4 yds. ⅝" cording
⅓ yd. 44/45"-wide red corduroy fabric (to cover cording)
Thread to match fabrics
Two 16" x 16" pillow forms **or** polyester filling
High-quality washable felt scraps: red, royal blue, flesh, white, black, gold
Thread to match sweaters and felt scraps
9" x 12" piece gray felt (for base of appliqué)
½ yd. Pellon® Wonder-Under™ Transfer Web
¼ yd. Pellon® Stretch-Ease™ **or** Sof-Shape™ interfacing
½ yd. ⅛"-wide green satin ribbon
6 black seed beads (for soldiers' eyes)
Twenty-two 4mm gold beads (7 for drum, 15 for soldiers)
Sewing machine with zipper foot
Measuring tape
Hand-sewing needle
Scissors

Note: Materials listed will make two pillows.

1. Enlarge both patterns proportionally on copy machine until soldiers are 9" tall. Appliqué pillow tops, following directions for sweaters and omitting interfacing used on inside of sweaters.

2. To make cording for **one** pillow, cut red corduroy fabric across grain into two 3" x 45" strips. Sew strips together along one 3" side to make one long strip. Stitch one end of cord to one end of corduroy strip, placing cord on wrong side of strip and centering. Fold corduroy strip around

cord, placing wrong sides of fabric together and aligning raw edges. Pin as needed to get started. Place cording under zipper foot with raw edges to the right. Machine stitch close to cord, being careful not to crowd cord. As you near end of cord, remove work from machine, hold loose end of cord firmly, and push fabric toward stitched end to create a shirred effect. Place work in machine again and continue to end of fabric. Repeat for cording for second pillow.

3. Run a stitching line 1" in from edge around perimeter of each pillow top. Place covered cording around perimeter of each pillow top with raw edge of cording toward raw edge of pillow top. Align stitching line on cording with stitching line on pillow front. Machine stitch cording to each pillow front, using zipper foot and following stitching line.

4. Pin each pillow front to a pillow back with right sides together and sew around perimeter along stitching line, leaving open at bottom. Trim seams, clip corners, and turn. Insert pillow form or polyester filling and blind stitch opening closed.

Happy Holidays Reindeer

Note: A general materials list is given for these projects. Specific materials and instructions for each project are listed separately. For reindeer projects utilizing Pellon® Wonder-Under™, follow manufacturer's instructions for fusing. For a large area, repeat fusing process, overlapping areas pressed, until all fabric is fused. For added stability, machine stitch around edges of deer on Ultrasuede® projects, such as the *Prancing Reindeer Sweatshirt* and both belts.

General materials:
Sewing machine with open-toe embroidery foot
Measuring tape
Scissors
Hand-sewing needle
Pencil
Tweezers
Iron

Happy Reindeer Gift Bags
Materials:
Red gift bag
Brown grocery bag paper **or** white paper
18"-length ⅛"-wide green ribbon
2 mini jingle bells
Glue stick **or** spray glue
Fine line marker

1. Trace reindeer pattern onto paper and cut out.

2. Using glue stick or spray glue (liquid white glue will make paper wrinkle), attach reindeer to bag, placing as desired.
3. Add details to reindeer with fine line marker, referring to photo on page 113. Glue on bow and jingle bell at each reindeer's neck.

Lined Reindeer Belt
Materials:
8" x 45" piece red fabric (for belt)
8" x 45" piece interfacing (if fabric is lightweight)
Lining to match fabric
Thread to match fabric
5" x 10" scrap tan Ultrasuede®
5" x 10" piece Pellon® Wonder-Under™ Transfer Web
2½" piece Velcro® (for closure)
2 black seed beads (for eyes)
20" fine gold braid

1. Trace belt pattern, adjusting as indicated on pattern to fit waist and aligning belt sides and ends with belt front.
Note: Total length of belt should be waist measurement plus 4".
2. Cut out belt, lining, and interfacing. Attach interfacing to wrong side of belt fabric. With right sides of belt fabric and lining together and raw edges aligned, sew belt, using a ¼" seam allowance and leaving an opening for turning. Turn, press, and slip stitch opening closed.
3. Trace reindeer pattern onto paper side of Wonder-Under™ and fuse to tan Ultrasuede®. Cut out reindeer and fuse to center front of belt. Tie gold braid in bows, and tack at reindeers' necks.
4. Sew Velcro® at belt ends for closure.

Prancing Reindeer Paper Garland
Materials:
5" x 50" piece brown kraft paper
Fine line markers: red, green
Paper clips
Fine, paper-cutting scissors

1. Fold paper accordion-style, making a fold every 9⅛". Use paper clips at edges to hold paper layers together.
2. Trace reindeer pattern onto paper and cut out, cutting antler area first. Do not cut ends of back legs; leave attached at paper folds, as indicated by broken lines on pattern. Unfold paper and, using markers, draw on eyes and bows.

Prancing Reindeer Sweatshirt
Materials:
Purchased sweatshirt
½"-wide woven braid in holiday colors (enough to fit around sweatshirt neck and cuffs)
Three 5" x 5" scraps tan Ultrasuede®, Doe Suede, **or** calico

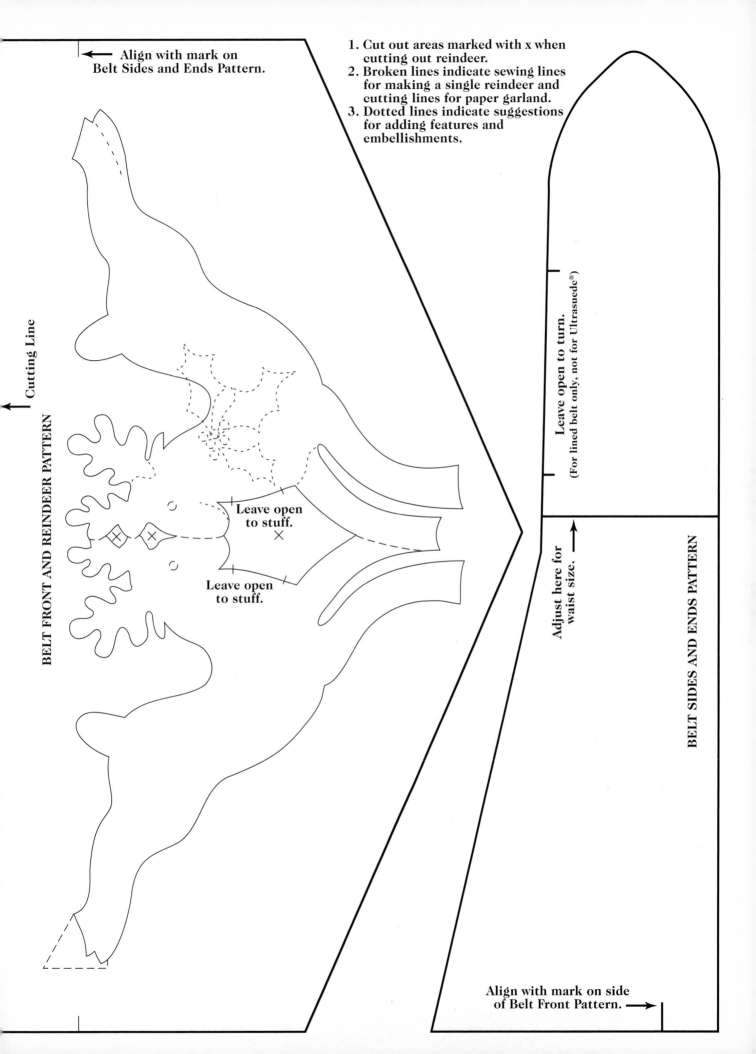

← Align with mark on
Belt Sides and Ends Pattern.

1. Cut out areas marked with x when cutting out reindeer.
2. Broken lines indicate sewing lines for making a single reindeer and cutting lines for paper garland.
3. Dotted lines indicate suggestions for adding features and embellishments.

Cutting Line →

BELT FRONT AND REINDEER PATTERN

Leave open to stuff.

Leave open to stuff.

Leave open to turn.
(For lined belt only, not for Ultrasuede®)

Adjust here for waist size. →

BELT SIDES AND ENDS PATTERN

Align with mark on side of Belt Front Pattern. →

5" x 15" piece Pellon® Wonder-Under™ Transfer Web
Black embroidery floss (for eyes)
White DMC #5 coton perlé (for snowflakes)
Thread to match braid and reindeer
1 yd. ⅛"-wide red/white polka-dot ribbon
1 yd. ⅛"-wide green/white polka-dot ribbon
3 mini jingle bells

1. Trace single reindeer pattern three times onto paper side of Wonder-Under™. Fuse Wonder-Under™ to wrong side of suede and cut out reindeer shapes. Fuse reindeer shapes to shirt front, referring to photo on page 112 for placement.
2. Use black floss to make a French knot for **each** reindeer's eye.
3. Use white coton perlé to make snowflakes, referring to photo on page 112 for placement.
Note: Each snowflake consists of six ½"-long straight stitches with a French knot at the end of each.
4. Sew braid around sweatshirt neck and cuffs.
5. Combine red and green ribbon as one. Tie a bow at one end of ribbon and tack at first reindeer's neck. Divide remaining ribbon into two equal parts to find approximate spot in ribbon to tie next bow. Tie bow and tack at middle reindeer's neck. There will be a loose loop of ribbon between the three reindeer. Repeat for the remaining reindeer. Tack a jingle bell at center of each bow.

Reindeer Necklace And Scarf Slide
Materials:
Two 5" x 10" scraps tan Ultrasuede® **or** Doe Suede
20"-length ⅛"-wide ribbon: red **or** green
22" black rattail cord (for necklace)
Thread to match suede
Polyester filling
5" x 10" piece freezer paper
Sharp, fine-bladed scissors
2 mini jingle bells (optional)
2 black seed beads (optional)
#7 **or** 60 sewing machine needle

1. Trace reindeer pattern onto papery side of freezer paper. Do not cut out. Place two pieces of suede with wrong sides together. Fuse slick side of freezer paper to right side of top piece of suede, using a dry iron on wool setting. Freezer paper will adhere to fabric and can be peeled off after sewing.
2. Set sewing-machine stitch length to approximately 24 stitches per inch. Using #7 or 60 needle and open-toe embroidery foot, sew through paper and Ultrasuede® layers, following traced line

on paper and leaving opening for stuffing as marked. Sew slowly to achieve a smooth line. To turn sharp corners, leave needle in fabric, lift presser foot, and pivot work. "Walk" machine around tiny antler area, hand-turning the handwheel of your machine.
3. Peel off freezer paper. Carefully cut out reindeer, leaving a 1/16"-⅛" seam allowance.
4. Use tweezers or the blunt end of a rug-yarn-sized needle to push polyester filling into reindeer. Use tiny amounts of filling at a time. Begin by lightly stuffing front legs, then stuff remainder of reindeer, concentrating most of the filling in the body and head areas. Filling will not fit into tips of antlers. Machine stitch openings closed.
5. Sew beads on for eyes or make French knots. Tie on ribbon bows around necks. Add small jingle bells or beads at bow centers, if desired.
6. To finish as a necklace, whipstitch rattail cord to back side of **each** reindeer's hind legs. To use as a scarf slide, pull ends of scarf through opening under reindeer's chins.

Reindeer Pin
Materials:
Two 5" x 5" scraps tan Ultrasuede® or Doe Suede
Thread to match
10" gold/silver braid (for bow)
Polyester filling
5" x 5" piece freezer paper
Black seed bead (optional)
1½" sew-on pin back

1. Follow instructions #1-#5 for *Reindeer Necklace And Scarf Slide*, except trace one reindeer facing direction of your choice onto papery side of freezer paper.
2. Hand-sew pin back on back side of reindeer.

Ultrasuede® Reindeer Belt
Materials:
Two 6" x 45" pieces black Ultrasuede®
5" x 10" scrap tan Ultrasuede®
Tiny scraps green Ultrasuede® (for holly)
6" x 55" piece Pellon® Wonder-Under™ Transfer Web
⅓ yd. gold braid
2½" black Velcro® (for closure)
2 black seed beads (for eyes)
10 red seed beads (for holly berries)
Fine line permanent marker

1. Trace belt pattern, adjusting as indicated on pattern to fit waist.
Note: Total length of belt should be waist measurement plus 4".
2. Cut two belt pieces from black suede.

Place pieces with wrong sides together, and use Wonder-Under™ to fuse the two pieces together.
3. Trace reindeer onto Wonder-Under™. Fuse Wonder-Under™ to wrong side of tan suede. Cut out reindeer and fuse to center of belt front.
4. Sew on black beads for eyes. Fuse holly leaves onto reindeer at necks, referring to pattern. Sew five red beads on each set of leaves for holly berries. Sew on gold bows.
5. Use fine line marker to add details to reindeer, if desired.
6. Sew Velcro® at belt ends for closure.

Quick & Easy Appliqué
Materials:
Purchased sweatshirts **or** long-sleeved T-shirts
Pre-made place mat and napkin sets
Assorted fabric scraps (for appliqué)
1 yd. 44"/45"-wide muslin (for pillow)
Thread to match muslin and fabric scraps
1/6 yd. 44"/45"-wide fabric (for **each** napkin ring)
Polyester filling (for pillow)
Pellon® Wonder-Under™ Transfer Web
Fabric stiffener **or** solution of 2 parts white glue to 1 part water (for napkin ring)
Small red buttons (for holly berries)
Gold and silver metallic rickrack
Glitter paint for fabric (available at craft stores)
6mm jingle bells (optional)
Sewing machine with zigzag stitch and appliqué foot
Measuring tape
Pencil
Scissors
Hand-sewing needle
Iron

Note: To ensure colorfastness, be sure to prewash all purchased items and fabric to be used for appliquéing before beginning. Follow manufacturer's instructions for fusing with Pellon® Wonder-Under™.

Shirts And Table Linens
1. Trace desired pattern shapes onto paper side of Wonder-Under™.
2. Fuse Wonder-Under™ to wrong side of fabric for appliqué.
3. Cut out shapes, following tracing lines.
Note: No seam allowance is needed for machine appliqué.
4. Peel paper backing from Wonder-Under™ and arrange pattern shapes as desired on shirts and table linens, referring to photos on pages 114 and 115. Fuse pattern shapes to shirts and table linens.
5. Machine appliqué around edges, trimming threads as you go.

Place pattern on fold line of fabric.

Suggestions: For Christmas tree with packages, hand sew jingle bells on tree for ornaments. Paint star and garland on tree and paint bows on packages. For holly leaf designs, arrange leaf shapes with several stems overlapping each other. Appliqué. Hand sew small red buttons for holly berries where stems overlap. When appliquéing holly design to table linens, arrange design so that buttons will not interfere with tableware, especially glasses. For packages with glitter paint, straight stitch around edges of package designs. Machine stitch rickrack on packages for ribbons and tack on handmade rickrack bows. Paint package edges with glitter paint, being sure to cover raw edges of fabric with paint.

Wreath Of Holly Pillow
Finished size: 15" x 15", including ruffle.
Note: Use a ¾" seam allowance.

1. Cut two 13½" x 13½" squares muslin for pillow front and back.
2. For preparation and appliquéing, follow instructions #1-#5 for shirts and table linens, arranging holly leaves on pillow front in wreath pattern or other design of your choice.
3. Sew on buttons for holly berries.
4. To make ruffle, mark and cut 7½" wide strips from remaining muslin. Seam strips together until ruffle measures at least 72". Seam ends together to make one continuous ruffle piece and press seams. Fold in half lengthwise and press along fold line.
5. Run gathering stitch along raw-edge side of ruffle ⅜" in from edge of fabric and pull thread to gather.
6. Pin ruffle to pillow front along seam line, having raw edges even and adjusting ruffles evenly around perimeter of pillow front. Stitch ruffle to pillow front.

7. Pin pillow back to pillow front with right sides together and stitch along seam line, leaving an opening in one side for turning.
8. Trim seams, clip corners, and turn pillow right-side out.
9. Stuff with polyester filling. Whipstitch opening closed.

Fabric Napkin Rings
Note: Fabric stiffener or glue and water solution can be made into a variety of consistencies which will change the stiffness of the completed project. Use less water in the solution for a very stiff finish or dilute stiffener or solution with water for a less stiff finish.

1. Cut one fabric strip 20" x 3" for bow and tails. Cut another strip 8" x 2" for ring and center of bow.
2. Work fabric stiffener into 20" x 3" piece with fingers.
3. Fold lengthwise edges to middle and hang to dry. Let dry approximately 45 minutes or until fabric is stiff but not brittle and still damp to the touch.
4. Measure 2½" to 3" in from one end of 8" x 2" piece and cut. Longer piece will be ring, shorter piece will be center of bow.
5. When bow piece is almost ready, dip center and ring pieces into fabric stiffener and work stiffener into fabric. Fold lengthwise edges as before and set center piece aside. Overlap fabric ends of ring piece to form loop. Hold piece until ends bond and set aside. Fold ends of bow piece to middle to form bow loops and tails. Place ring piece in center of bow on back side, making sure overlapped portion of ring piece touches bow so it will be hidden when project is finished. Hold bow and ring pieces together at center and wrap with center of bow piece, hiding overlap on back side, as before. Hold until firmly bonded and set aside to dry thoroughly.

Pearly Sheep

Materials:
Purchased pullover sweater
Thread to match
Thread in contrasting color
3½ yds. 3mm fixed strung pearls (cannot be unstrung)
2 tiny star sequins (for eyes)
2 black seed beads (for eyes)
½ yd. ¾"-wide black/white polka-dot ribbon
Scraps of black Ultrasuede®
Scraps of Pellon® Wonder-Under™ Transfer Web
10" x 10" square lightweight iron-on interfacing

Patterns for gold T-shirt

Patterns for red T-shirt

Paper
Measuring tape
Straight pins
Hand-sewing needle
Scissors
Pencil
Iron

1. Transfer pattern to paper and cut out pattern. Pin pattern to sweater and carefully try on sweater to be sure placement of sheep is complementary. Using contrasting thread, sew a temporary outline around paper pattern. Remove pattern. To reinforce design area, turn sweater inside out and fuse iron-on interfacing to wrong side of sweater over outline area.
2. Trace sheep heads, ears, legs, and tail onto paper side of Wonder-Under™.
Note: Pattern pieces for Ultrasuede® parts of sheep must be placed wrong-side up when tracing onto paper side of Wonder-Under™. They will appear to be back-

wards, but this is correct as the process for fusing with Wonder-Under™ will reverse the fabric pieces.
Following manufacturer's instructions, fuse Wonder-Under™ to back of Ultrasuede®. Cut out Ultrasuede® pieces and fuse to sweater.
3. Cut pearls into 1½" lengths a few lengths at a time. Pin in curlicues and stitch to sweater with matching thread, filling in the sheep shape. Remove temporary outline threads. Tack on sequins and beads for eyes.
4. Pin then stitch long pearl curlicues from shoulder opposite sheep, referring to photo on page 116 for placement. Tie ribbon into a bow and tack on at top of shoulder curlicues.
Option: Choose a sweater or sweatshirt in a light color and paint on sheep face, ears, legs, and tail. To finish, squeeze Delta Shiny Stuff™ or Glitter Stuff™ into curlicue shapes in place of pearls.

HO HO HO Sweater

DMC	Color
· white	white
∕ 762	pearl gray, vy. lt.
v 415	pearl gray
✳ 318	steel gray, lt.
■ 310	black
↙ 3328	salmon, med.
6 666	red, bt.
9 321	red
▲ 304	red, med.
● 699	green

3	700	green, bt.
o	761	salmon, lt.
=	754	peach flesh, lt.
I	948	peach flesh, vy. lt.
\	729	old gold, med.
−	676	old gold, lt.

Sweater: Navy stockinette-stitch sweater
Stitch count: 70H x 134W
Instructions: Work duplicate stitch using six strands of floss. (See illustration.) Backstitch lines are for cross stitch only. Use three strands 318 for Santa's face.

Placement instructions: Center design ¼" up from bottom of sweater. Repeat border design to side seams to accommodate for different sweater sizes. Stitch border design around sleeves and 1" down from neckband.

132

Shaded portion indicates overlap from previous page.

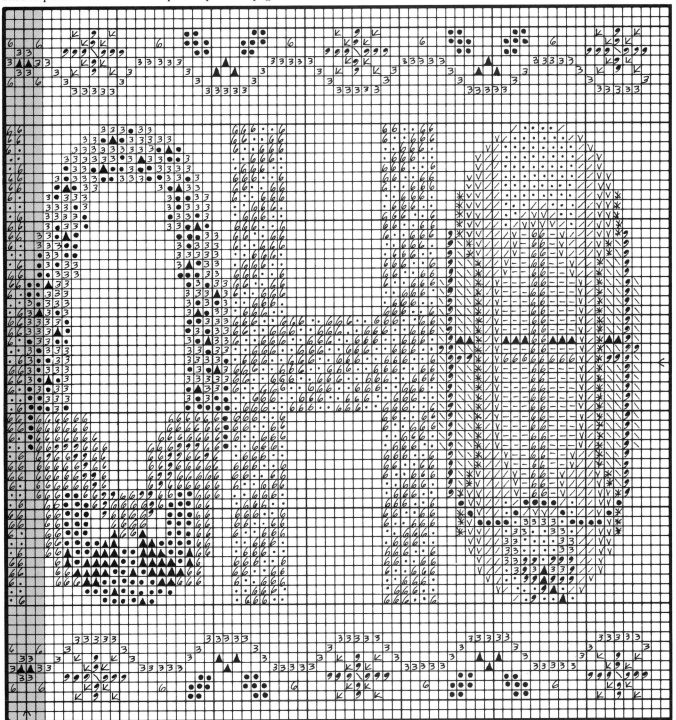

DUPLICATE STITCH INSTRUCTIONS

Step 1—Thread needle and tie a knot at end of floss. Anchor floss on back of sweater, looping thread several times before beginning. Insert needle from back and bring through to right side of sweater in the center of a stitch.

Step 2—Slip needle under two threads of stitch above and draw through.

Step 3—To complete stitch, insert needle in hole where stitch began. This represents one square on chart.

DUPLICATE STITCH

133

Sheep In A Row Sweatshirt

KNITTING ABBREVIATIONS

dec—decrease
k—knit
rnd—round
rpt—repeat from * to *
st(s)—stitch(es)
tog—together

Materials:
Ruler
Washable marking pencil
#18 tapestry needle
Crochet hook, size D
Scissors
Knitting markers
6 yds. #3 coton perlé, DMC light blue 800
24" circular needles #4 (**or** size required

to obtain gauge of 5 stitches per inch)
Sweatshirt; light blue, **or** other color of your choice
16" circular needles (two sizes smaller than 24" circular needles) for neck band
Unger Plantation cotton sportweight yarn:
   76 yds. #207, light blue (color *A*)
   71 yds. #800, white (color *B*)
   23 yds. #307, light pink (color *C*)
   22 yds. #119, pale yellow (color *D*)
Brunswick Moonbeam cotton sportweight yarn:
   14 yds. #8506, black (color *E*)
Measuring tape
Scissors

Note: Please read all instructions carefully before beginning. Yokes are worked in the round on circular needles. When changing colors, bring the new color under the old color to avoid a hole. Illustrations for color pattern knitting are worked from the bottom up and each row is worked from right to left. Repeat design area between solid black lines (on illustrations) as many times as necessary to fit your yoke. Gauge is calculated at 5 stitches per inch; however, exact gauge is not critical. This also applies to number of decrease rounds, so stitches need not come out even. (This may be the only time when close is good enough!)

1. On sweatshirt, measure 4" down from bottom of neck band around entire yoke, marking with washable marking pencil.
2. Cut out yoke along markings.
3. Use coton perlé and tapestry needle to work chain st approximately ¼" apart (4 sts per inch) and ¾" down from cut edge. Begin chain st at left back shoulder seam and work around entire yoke.
4. Begin at back left seam line, use crochet hook to pull loops of color *A* under each chain st, and place on 24" needle. Place marker. K one rnd. Dec if necessary to obtain even number of sts.
Rnd 1 with A k
Rnd 2 *k1A, k1B, rpt from *
Rnd 3 *k1B, k1A, rpt from *
Rnd 4 *k1A, k1B, rpt from *
Rnd 5 *k1B, k1A, rpt from *
Rnd 6 with A k
Rnd 7 with C k
Rnd 8 with B k
Rnd 9 with C k, dec as necessary to obtain number of sts evenly divisible by 6
Rnd 10-16 (Ill. 1) (colors *B* and *D*)
Rnd 17 with A k
Rnd 18 with A *k2, k2 tog, rpt from *
Rnd 19-29 (Ill. 2) (colors *A*, *B*, and *E*) (On rnd 19, dec as necessary to obtain number of sts evenly divisible by 9)
Rnd 30 with A k
Rnd 31 with A *k1, k2 tog, rpt from *
Rnd 32 with B k, dec as necessary to obtain number of sts evenly divisible by 7
Rnd 33-37 (Ill. 3) (colors *B* and *C*)
Rnd 38 with B k

Neck band: With 16" circular needles and A, k, dec 8-14 sts, evenly spaced around, depending on size. Continue k until neck band measures approximately 1¾". Bind off loosely.

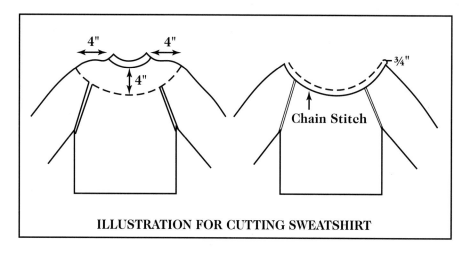

ILLUSTRATION FOR CUTTING SWEATSHIRT

ILL. 1
□   Color *B*
●   Color *D*

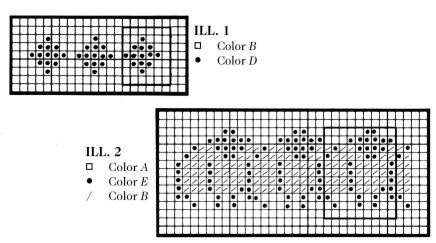

ILL. 2
□   Color *A*
●   Color *E*
/   Color *B*

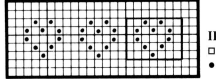

ILL. 3
□   Color *B*
●   Color *C*

134

Mad For Plaid

Note: A general materials list is given for these projects. Specific materials and instructions for each project are listed separately.

General materials:
Sewing machine with zigzag stitch
Measuring tape
Polyester filling
Scissors
Hand-sewing needle
Straight pins
Pencil
Iron
Paper

Plaid Stars
Materials:
7" x 14" piece plaid flannel
Thread to match
10" piece ⅛"-wide complementary ribbon
   (for hanger)
Five 10-mm jingle bells (optional)
Hand-sewing needle with large eye

Note: Materials listed will make one star. Each star measures approximately 5½" across.

1. Transfer Star Pattern and cut out. Pattern line is seam line. Fold flannel with right sides together, place pattern atop folded fabric, and pin. Trace around pattern and mark opening. Remove pat-

tern from fabric. Sew around star, using very small stitches on sewing machine, following tracing line, and leaving an opening for turning as marked. Cut out star, leaving a 3/16" seam allowance.
2. Clip inner corners and clip off points. Turn stars right-side out and stuff lightly. Blind stitch opening closed.
3. Thread needle with ribbon and sew through one point of star. Tack jingle bells on ends of star points, if desired.

Super Quick Plaid Gifts
Materials:
2 purchased hand towels
Assorted complementary plaid scraps
Thread: green, red, gold
Scraps of Pellon® Wonder-Under™
   Transfer Web
¼"-wide gold braid (To determine amount needed for each towel, multiply width of towel by two and add 2".)
Five 7-mm jingle bells for each towel

Note: Materials listed will make **one** of each towel shown.

1. To finish towel with plaid band, cut a strip of plaid fabric measuring 2¾" x width of towel plus ½". Pin band across towel to form a border, turning raw edges under ¼" around perimeter of band and measuring from bottom of towel to achieve a straight band. Sew close to edges around perimeter of band. Remove pins. Zigzag a row of gold braid at top and bottom of band, turning raw edge ends under ¼".
2. To finish towel with plaid star, trace pattern onto paper side of Wonder-Under™ and fuse to wrong side of plaid, following manufacturer's instructions for fusing. Cut out star, remove paper, and fuse to towel, referring to photo on page 121 for placement. Machine satin stitch around edges of star. Tack a tiny jingle bell at each star point.

Cozy Flannel Pillowcases
Materials:
1 yd. 44/45"-wide red plaid flannel fabric
1 yd. 44/45"-wide blue plaid flannel fabric
2 yds. ⅝"-wide red satin ribbon (for red plaid pillowcase)
2 yds. 1"-wide green grosgrain ribbon (for blue plaid pillowcase)
2 yds. 1"-wide blue grosgrain ribbon (for blue plaid pillowcase)
2 yds. ¼"-wide metallic silver braid (for blue plaid pillowcase)

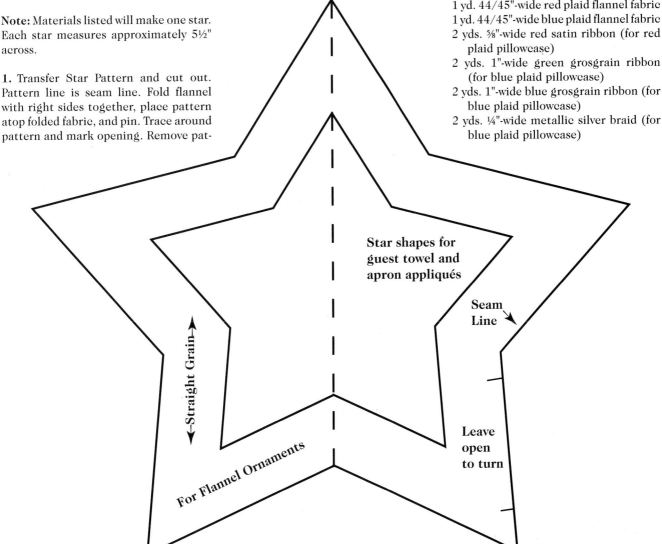

Star shapes for guest towel and apron appliqués

Seam Line

Leave open to turn

Straight Grain

For Flannel Ornaments

4 star-shaped thread appliqués (for red plaid pillowcase)
Thread: red, blue, green, gold, silver **or** gray

Note: Materials listed will make pillowcases shown. Standard size pillowcase measurement is 21" x 31".

1. Prewash and iron plaid flannel fabric. Fold fabric in half lengthwise with right sides together. Sew across 22½" end and down 36" side, using a 1" seam allowance. Serge or clean finish seams.
2. At open end, turn flannel under 1" and press to form finished edge. Turn flannel under 3" to form hem. Stitch hem.
3. Turn pillowcase right-side out.
4. To finish, sew ribbon and braid trim around pillowcase at open end, beginning and ending at center of one side (this side will be top of pillowcase) and leaving a tail of ribbon at both beginning and end for tying a bow. Refer to photo on page 119 for placement.
Note: Ribbon on red pillowcase begins 2¼" from open end edge. Ribbons on blue pillowcase begin 1¼" from open-end edge. Tie ribbon ends into a bow. Tack star appliqués to red plaid pillowcase, referring to photo on page 119 for placement.

Wool Tartan Pillows With Gift Tags
Materials:
½ yd. 44/45"-wide plaid wool fabric
2⅝ yds. ⅞"-wide complementary ribbon
14" x 14" square pillow form
3" x 9" piece white felt
Delta Shiny Stuff™: red, blue
Delta Glitter Stuff™: green
Green fabric or felt scrap (for tag with Christmas tree)
Scraps of Pellon® Wonder-Under™ Transfer Web
7" piece metallic gold cord
Hand-sewing needle with large eye

Note: Materials listed will make **one** pillow and **one** gift tag.

Tree for gift tag on *Wool Tartan Pillows*

1. Cut two pieces from plaid wool fabric, **each** 15" square. Place pieces with right sides together and sew around perimeter, using a ½" seam allowance and leaving an 8" opening in one side for turning. Trim seams, clip corners, and turn right-side out. Insert pillow form and blind stitch opening closed. Tie on ribbon as for a package, referring to photo on page 121.
2. To make gift tags, fold felt in half lengthwise. Fuse felt to itself for double thickness, using Wonder-Under™ for fusing. Cut to 2¾" x 4½" and trim one end to a point, referring to photo on page 121. Use Shiny Stuff™ to write Christmas greetings on tags. Use Glitter Stuff™ to make holly leaf shapes. Add red dots for berries. For tag with tree shape, trace tree shape onto paper side of Wonder-Under™, fuse onto green fabric or felt scrap, and cut out. Fuse green tree onto tag. To finish, thread needle with gold cord, knot one end, and sew through pointed end of tag. Tie other end of cord onto pillow bow.

Holiday Apron
Materials:
Purchased apron
Assorted complementary plaid fabric scraps
Scraps of Pellon® Wonder-Under™ Transfer Web
Delta Glitter Stuff™: gold

1. Trace patterns onto paper side of Wonder-Under™ and fuse to wrong side of plaid fabric, following manufacturer's instructions. Cut out stars, remove paper, and fuse to apron, as desired.
2. Use Delta Glitter Stuff™ to secure star edges and to add gold dots, as desired.

Button-on Pillows
Materials:
1 yd. 44/45"-wide red corduroy fabric
½ yd. 44/45" wide black/white houndstooth-check wool fabric (for button-on patches)
Two 14"-square pillow forms
7"-square piece white fabric (for horse)
Green Ultrasuede® scraps (for saddle, rocker, and holly leaves)
Red fabric scraps (for mane and holly berries)
9" x 5" piece gold lamé (for horn)
Two 14" squares black felt (for backing and binding edges of patches)
1 yd. Pellon® Wonder-Under™ Transfer Web
Eight ¾"-diameter flat gold buttons

Red embroidery floss (for horse's tail)
Black seed bead (for horse's eye)
¼"-wide gold braid and 1/16"-wide gold cord scraps (for bridle, reins, and stirrup)
Thread: red, green, white, black, gold

Note: Materials listed will make **one** of **each** pillow shown.

1. Cut two 11" squares from houndstooth-check fabric. Cut four 15" squares from red corduroy fabric.
2. Place two corduroy squares with right sides together and sew around edges, using a ½" seam allowance and leaving an 8" opening in one side for turning. Clip corners and turn. Insert pillow form and blind stitch opening closed.
3. Trace patterns for horse, rocker, saddle, mane, holly leaves, berries, and horn onto paper side of Wonder-Under™, grouping pattern pieces for items of like colors. Fuse shapes to proper color fabric, referring to materials list and photo on page 122. Cut out shapes, arrange, and fuse to 11" square of houndstooth-check fabric, again referring to photo on page 122 as a guide and following manufacturer's instructions for fusing. Machine satin stitch around horn, horse, saddle, and rocker, using matching thread. Topstitch veins on leaves, lines on mane, and across tops of berries, as indicated by dotted lines on pattern pieces. To make horse's tail, tack one looped end of skein of embroidery floss at X, trim loops from opposite end, and trim loose ends to approximately 4". Tack gold braid and cord in place for bridle, reins, and stirrup, referring to photo on page 122 for placement.
4. Cut two 10¾" squares of Wonder-Under™ and fuse to wrong side of each houndstooth-check square. Remove paper from Wonder-Under™ and center houndstooth-check square right-side up atop 14" black felt square. Fuse. Measure and trim felt to ⅝" larger all around than houndstooth-check square. Fold and press felt to front of houndstooth-check square to form binding. Pin and stitch in place.
5. Place buttons on each houndstooth-check pillow patch to determine pleasing position. Mark and make four vertical buttonholes. Center houndstooth-check patches on red pillows and mark position for buttons. Sew buttons onto pillows and button patches to pillows.

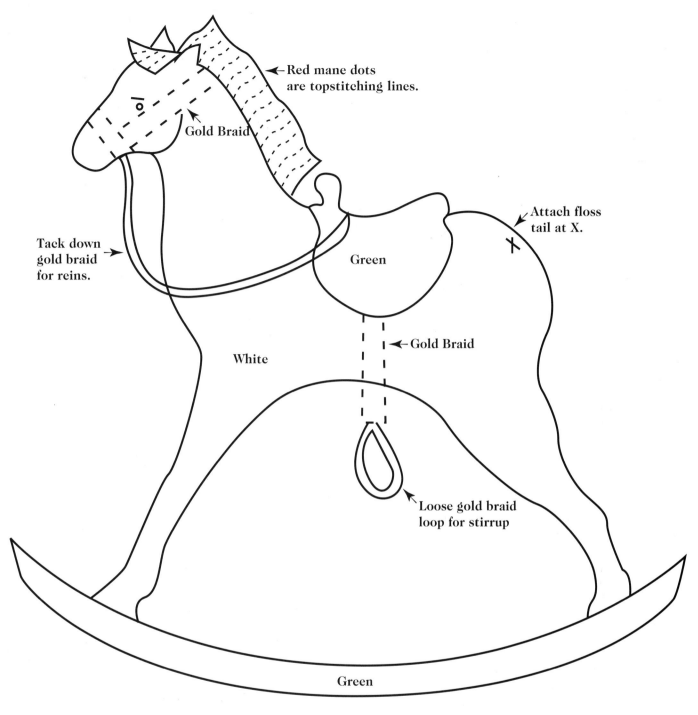

← Red mane dots
are topstitching lines.

Gold Braid

Tack down
gold braid
for reins. →

Attach floss
tail at X. →

Green

← Gold Braid

White

Loose gold braid
loop for stirrup

Green

BUTTON-ON PILLOW

Holiday Finery
Materials:
Fashion fabric of your choice (for skirt—
  see note to determine amount needed.)
Thread to match
1¾"- to 2"-wide complementary ribbon
  (for waistband—see #4 to determine
  amount needed.)
Two ⅞" buttons (to cover)
Paper **or** permanent pattern material

Note: To determine amount of fabric
needed for this pleated, wrap skirt, measure your waist. Multiply your waist measurement times two and add 19". This is
the amount of fabric you will need to
pleat top of skirt, including hems. If
fabric can be used crosswise (i.e. if selvage edge can be parallel to hem or if
fabric is a border print), this is the number of inches of fabric to buy. (See Ill. 1

on page 139.) If fabric has a design that
requires it to be used lengthwise (i.e. if
selvage edges need to be parallel to sides),
purchase two to three times the length
you wish skirt to be, plus 2½" per length
(2" for hem and ½" for seam allowance at
top). Whether you need two or three
times the length will be determined by
your waist measurement. (See Ills. 2 and
2A on page 139.) If fabric is 45" wide, two

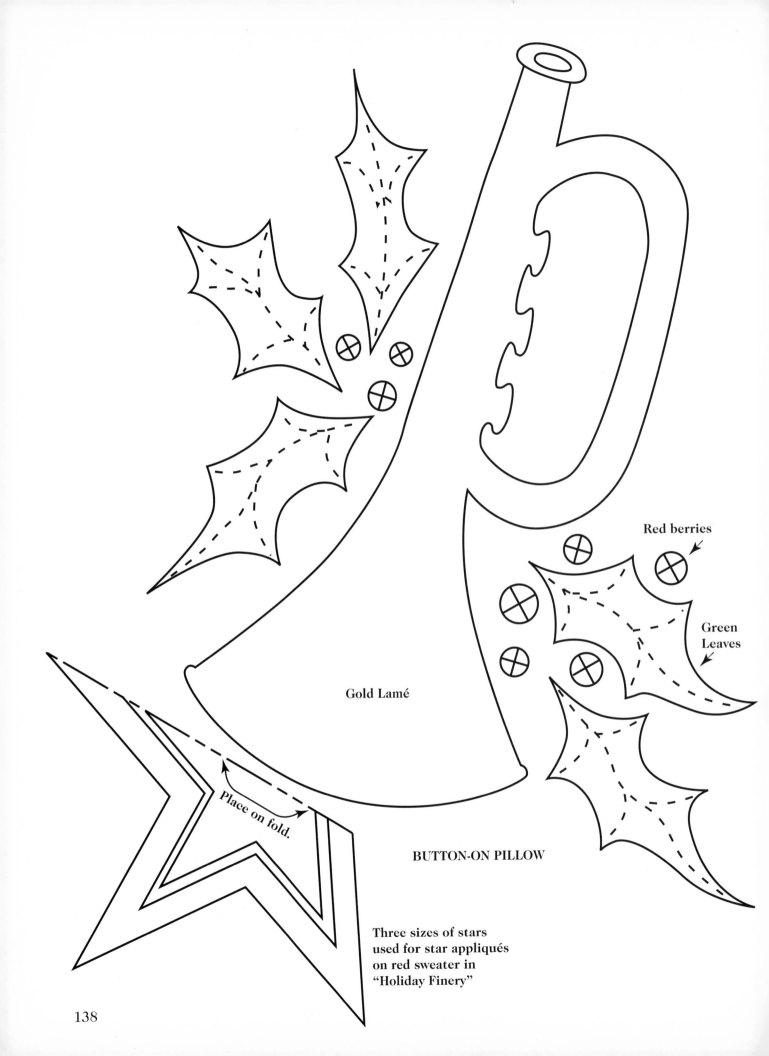

Red berries

Green
Leaves

Gold Lamé

Place on fold.

BUTTON-ON PILLOW

Three sizes of stars
used for star appliqués
on red sweater in
"Holiday Finery"

times the desired length total, cut in half crosswise and sewn together at selvage edges, will give you 90" to pleat. If your waist times two plus 19" is less than 90", two lengths will be enough. If the measurement is more than 90", purchase an additional length and sew to the other two at selvage to equal 135" to pleat. (See Ill. 3.)

1. To make permanent pattern, refer to Ill. 4. Cut a piece of paper or permanent pattern material into a rectangle with side A equalling waist times two plus 19" and side B equalling your desired skirt length plus 2½". Along side A, mark hems and pleating lines as indicated on illustration. Mark the 2" hem and 4" spaces at each edge first, then measure off pleats, leaving 2" between a and b. If last pleat does not fit, leave unpleated and add to 4" area. (This area will be under skirt overlap in front.) Pin pleats on pattern as shown (Ill. 5 on page 140), matching a to b, and try on pattern. Pattern should overlap (wrap) about 10" in front. (See Ill. 6 on page 140.) Adjust pattern if necessary by adding or deleting pleats.
2. Unpin pleats in pattern. Pin pattern

across top of single thickness of fabric. Cut out skirt. Fold, pin, and staystitch pleats.
3. Press fabric under 2" on each end and at bottom of skirt. Turn raw edge under ¼" to finish edge. Pin and sew hems.
4. Measure length of pleated waistline of skirt. Purchase ribbon two times this length (plus 1" for seam allowance) for waistband. Cut ribbon length in half. With right sides together, sew a ½" seam in each short end of ribbon. Turn ribbon right-side out. Sew the two pieces of ribbon together along one long edge with wrong sides together. Slip long open edge of ribbon down ½" over pleated raw edge of skirt, pin to skirt, baste, and sew.
5. Try on skirt and mark placement for two buttonholes in overlap portion of waistband and for two buttons in portion that wraps underneath. Cover buttons with fabric scraps from skirt. Sew buttonholes in overlap portion and buttons on portion that wraps underneath.

Star-Studded Sweater
Materials :
Purchased sweater of your choice **or** one from your closet

Thread to match
½ yd. Pellon® Wonder-Under™ Transfer Web
¼ yd. silver tissue lamé
Scraps from split skirt
½ yd. lightweight fusible interfacing

Note: Pattern used for split skirt shown is Simplicity 7174. If this pattern is unavailable in your area, substitute similar split skirt patterns by Simplicity or by other commercial pattern manufacturers.

1. Trace patterns onto paper side of Wonder-Under™, reversing at broken line to complete motif. Fuse to wrong side of fabric, following manufacturer's instructions.
2. Cut out stars and remove paper. Pin stars across top of sweater, referring to photo on page 120 for placement, and fuse, following manufacturer's instructions for fusing.
3. Iron lightweight interfacing behind stars on inside of sweater to stabilize sweater knit while satin stitching star edges. Sew a narrow satin stitch around edges of stars.

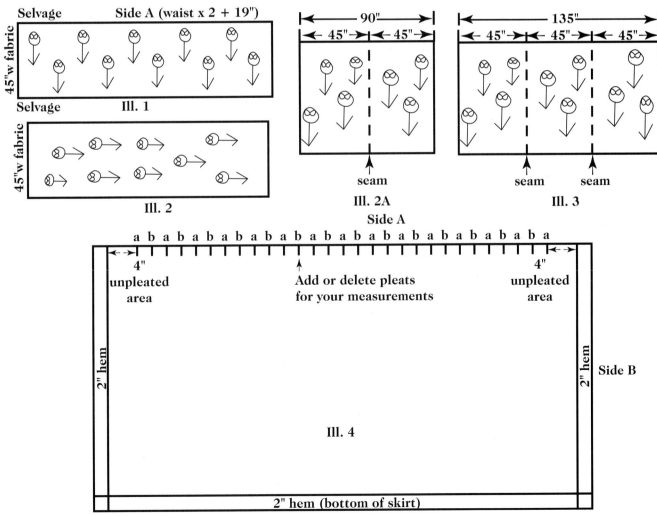

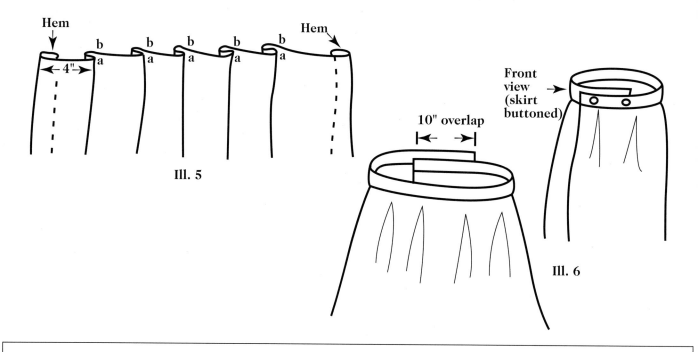

Ill. 5

10" overlap

Front view (skirt buttoned)

Ill. 6

How-Tos For Making Ornament Cording

To make cording trim for ornaments, you will need one skein of floss in the color of your choice for each ornament you wish to trim. When selecting floss colors, refer to color codes to achieve exact color matches.

Begin by unwinding entire skein of floss. Then bring the two raw ends together, dividing floss length in half, so that you have two main threads consisting of six strands each. Fold in half again, and then once more, smoothing each time as if folding a blanket. At this point, one end of floss will have raw edges, the other loops (Ill. 1). Tie a knot in the end with raw edges and loop over top of chair (Ill.2). To twist, insert fingers through center of looped end and move wrist in a circular motion (Ill.3). Continue twisting until floss tightens around fingers. Remove fingers until just one remains in floss. Remove from finger without letting go of twist in floss. Hand twist the remaining portion. Bring the two ends together again, holding securely and dividing in the middle with one finger (Ill. 4). Then remove end with raw edges from back of chair. Remove finger from middle dividing point. Floss will twist. When it stops twisting, run hand over length of floss several times to smooth, and tie a knot in raw-edge end to hold twist (Ill.5). Whipstitch to perimeter of ornaments, making a hanging loop at top of ornament or leaving a twisted-floss tail to attach an ornament hanger.

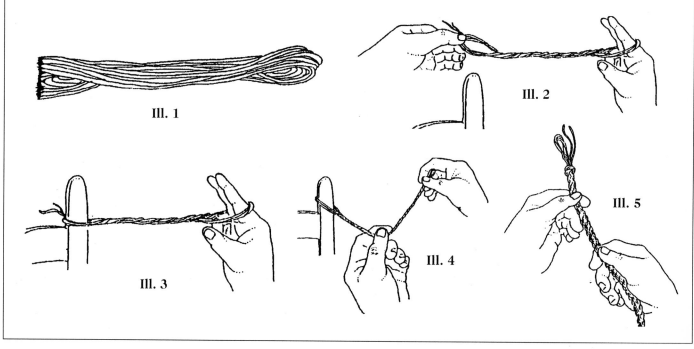

Ill. 1

Ill. 2

Ill. 3

Ill. 4

Ill. 5

General Instructions For Cross Stitch

Basic Supplies: Even-weave fabric, tapestry needle(s), six-strand embroidery floss, embroidery scissors, embroidery hoop (optional).

Fabric Preparation: The instructions and yardage for finishing materials have been written and calculated for each of the projects shown stitched on the fabric listed in each color code. Alternate fabric choices have also been listed. If you wish to stitch a design on an alternate fabric, or alter its placement, you will need to recalculate the finished size of the project, as well as the yardage of finishing materials needed, and make the necessary dimension adjustments when finishing.

Determine size of fabric needed for a project by dividing number of horizontal stitches by thread count of fabric. For example, if a design 35 stitches wide is worked on 14-count fabric, it will cover 2½" (35 divided by 14 equals 2½). Repeat process for vertical count. Add three inches on all sides of design area to find dimensions for cutting fabric. Whipstitch edges to prevent fraying.

Floss Preparation: Cut floss into 14" to 18" lengths. Separate all six strands. Reunite number of strands needed and thread needle, leaving one floss end longer than the other.

Where To Start: Start wherever you like! Some designers suggest finding center of fabric and starting there. Others recommend beginning with a central motif, while still others work borders first. Many find fabric center, count up and back to the left, and start with the uppermost left stitch. Wherever you begin, be sure to leave allowance for all horizontal and vertical stitches so that a 3" fabric margin is left around completed design.

Should you choose to begin at the center point, find it by folding fabric from top to bottom and then from left to right. Use a straight pin to mark upper-left corner at junction of folds, then unfold fabric. Pin will be in center of fabric.

After deciding where to begin on fabric, find same point on graph. Each square on graph represents one stitch. Those squares containing a symbol (i.e., X,T,O) indicate that a stitch should be made in that space over those threads. Different symbols represent different colors of floss for stitches. (See color code of chart.) They may also indicate partial or decorative stitches. Familiarize yourself with color code before you begin stitching. Even-weave fabric may be stretched over an embroidery hoop to facilitate stitching.

Stitching The Design: Using the illustrations on page 142, stitch design, completing all full and partial cross stitches first. Cross all full cross stitches in same direction to achieve a smooth surface appearance. Work backstitches second, and any decorative stitches last.

Helpful Hints For Stitching: Do not knot floss. Instead, catch end on back of work with first few stitches. As you stitch, pull floss through fabric "holes" with one stroke, not several short ones. The moment you feel resistance from floss, cease pulling. Consistent tension on floss results in a smoother look for stitches. Drop your needle frequently to allow floss to untwist. It twists naturally as you stitch and, as it gets shorter, must be allowed to untwist more often. To begin a new color on project, prepare floss and secure new strands as noted. To end stitching, run floss under several completed stitches and clip remaining strands close to surface. Many times it is necessary to skip a few spaces (threads) on the fabric in order to continue a row of stitches in the same color. If you must skip an area covering more than ¼", end stitching as described and begin again at next point. This procedure prevents uneven tension on the embroidery surface and snagging on back. It also keeps colors from showing through unstitched areas. Do not carry thread over an area that will remain unstitched.

When You Are Finished: For designs using cotton or linen floss on cotton or linen even-weave fabric, hand wash piece with mild detergent in warm water. Rinse thoroughly with cold water. Roll in terry towel and squeeze gently to remove excess moisture. Do not wring. Unroll towel and allow piece to dry until barely damp. Iron on padded surface with design face down, using medium setting for heat. A press cloth will help prevent shine on dark fabrics. **Note:** Acrylics, acrylic blends, wools or silks must be treated differently when cleaning. Check manufacturer's guidelines for special cleaning instructions.

Helpful Hints for Crafting

The instructions and yardage for finishing materials have been written and calculated for each of the projects shown and crafted from the materials listed. If you wish to craft a design using materials of different dimensions than those listed or to stitch a design on an alternate fabric or to alter its placement, you will need to recalculate the finished size of the project, as well as the yardage of finishing materials needed, and make the necessary dimension adjustments when purchasing supplies and making the projects. For general instructions for making ornament cording and for making a bow, refer to pages 140 and 105, respectively.

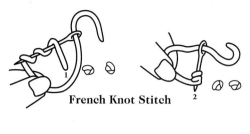

French Knot Stitch

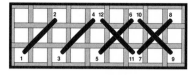

Full Cross Stitch (over one thread)

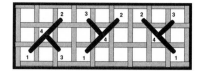

¼ Cross Stitch (over one thread)

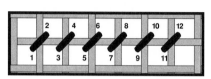

Full Cross Stitch (over two threads)

¾ Cross Stitch (over two threads)

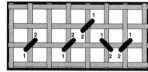

Lazy Daisy Stitch

Basic ½ Cross Stitch

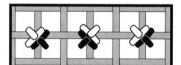

¾ Cross Stitches (over one in various positions)

¼ Cross Stitch (over two threads)

½ Cross Stitch (over two threads)

Two ¾ Stitches (in one square, using two different floss colors)

Backstitch (across two ¾ stitches and around full cross)

Basic Backstitch

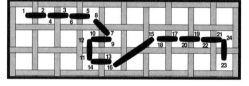

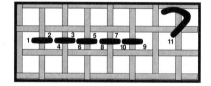

Backstitch (showing variations)

Shopper's Guide

Page 10—Copper #0308 Foil Art available from Zim's, Inc., Post Office Box 57620, Salt Lake City, UT 84107, 1-800-268-2505.

Page 37—*Original Christmas Tree* dinnerware by Cuthbertson; *Chantilly* stainless by Gorham.

Page 53—Majolica plate from Pier 1 Imports, Birmingham, Alabama; craft birds from Michael's, Birmingham, Alabama.

Page 77—13" arch candle rack available from Wheatland Crafts, Inc., 834 Scuffletown Road, Simpsonville, SC 29681, 1-800-334-7706

Page 94—Blue towel set by Avanti; Wisteria™ drawer sachet by Claire Burke®.

Page 110—Flag garland by Midwest Importers of Cannon Falls, Inc.

Page 112—Kreinik Metallic Braids available from The Daisy Chain, Post Office Box 1258, Parkersburg, WV 26102, (304)428-9500; Mill Hill Glass Seed Beads from Gay Bowles Sales, Inc.; Ultrasuede® scraps available from UltraMouse Ltd., 3433 Bennington Court, Birmingham, MI 48010. (Send LSASE + $1.50 for catalog.)

Page 120—Liz Claiborne blouse courtesy of Parisian, Inc., Birmingham, Alabama; shoes and headband courtesy of Macy's, Birmingham, Alabama.

Page 121—Wicker mirror and votive candles from Pier 1 Imports, Birmingham, Alabama; *Holiday* china by Lenox.

Items not appearing in "Shopper's Guide" are either commonly available, antiques, or from private collections.

Crafters And Designers

Index

Numbers in **bold** type indicate color photo pages. All other numbers refer to pages for charts, color codes, patterns, and instructions.